THE
NEW
TESTAMENT
EPISTLES

Analysis and Notes

by
VICTOR E. HOVEN

BAKER BOOK HOUSE
Grand Rapids 6, Michigan
1959

Library of Congress Catalog Card Number: 59-8341

Printed in United States of America

Foreword

This production is not a formal commentary, the usual style of which is verse by verse treatment. The author's effort is to point the way and thus assist the student to acquire a direct understanding of the word of God, and at the same time to leave ample room for him to use his own mind. The Bible is addressed to all men, hence can be understood by all — without a human interpreter. It should always be allowed to speak for itself.

This book has been prepared for the ordinary English student of the New Testament Letters. To that end there is a set purpose to avoid, as much as possible, technicalities arising from the original Greek text, leaving that to the classroom. The endeavor is simplicity and clarity, leading the student to personal application and appreciation of the divine word, and thus bringing him into the very presence of God, there to hear Him speak.

The method employed is analytic and synthetic. By analysis the subject matter of God's penmen is traced; by brief notes understanding is assisted; the final objective is growth in grace and knowledge unto salvation, II Pet. 3:18; I Pet. 2:2.

The title, *The New Testament Epistles,* carries a distinctive meaning to the Bible student. The book of Acts of Apostles contains the history of the first division of Christ's Commission to His Apostles (Matt. 28:19, 20), telling us how to "make disciples." Here we observe the motive, the message and the method of evangelism under the supervision of the Holy Spirit. The New Testament Epistles are concerned with the second part of the Commission — "teaching them." The divine purpose is a church intelligent in the Scriptures in order correctly to represent the only Savior and Head of the church to the world. To this end Paul labored to "present every man perfect in Christ."

V. E. H.

Contents

Letter to the Church at Rome

INTRODUCTION.

1. Author. Paul wrote this letter in A.D. 58, during his three months' stay at Corinth, Rom. 16:23; I Cor. 1:14; Acts 20:1-3. It appears that he sent the letter to Rome by Phoebe, a deaconess in the church at Cenchreae, Rom. 16:2.

2. Persons addressed. Though there were many Jews in the church, the majority seems to have been Gentiles, Rom. 1:13; 16:3-15. Origin of the church is obscure. It appears from 1:11-15, that Paul at this time had never been at Rome but Jews from there were at Jerusalem on the day of Pentecost, Acts 2:10, and some of them might have planted the church. Or those scattered by persecution following the death of Stephen might have traveled as far as Rome and preached there, Acts 8:1, 4.

3. Design.

a. Its place in the New Testament. Although it is not the first letter written by Paul, its place next to the book of Acts is logical, for it is a discussion of the grounds on which a sinner is justified before God. In Acts we are told *what* to do to be saved; in Romans we are told *why*.

b. Its purpose. (1) To prepare the church at Rome for Paul and his work. It would fortify the disciples against slanderous misrepresentations of him by his enemies and also dispose the church toward his work so that he could use it as a base of operation while in Spain, 15:24. (2) To set forth the relation of Jews and Gentiles to the gospel and thus settle all differences among them. They were prejudiced against each other. Moreover, the Judaizing group in the church would impose upon the Gentile believers some of the law of Moses. Paul settles the question by stating what the gospel really is, 1:16, 17; proves by

9

irresistible arguments that Jews and Gentiles are on equal footing before God, and that both need the gospel in order to be saved. This occasioned a review of Judaism in relation to Christianity, showing that Christ did what the law of Moses could not do. By means of this epistle Paul's strategy was to publish these facts in the capitol city, the effect of which would be felt in every Christian congregation throughout the empire, for all roads and travel led to Rome.

ANALYSIS AND NOTES

INTRODUCTION, 1:1-16.

1. Salutation, 1-7.

a. The writer, 1. In relation to Christ he is "bondservant," *doulos,* one who gives himself up wholly to another's will. See Matt. 25:21 for same word. In relation to the gospel he is "apostle"—one sent forth with a message. As such he was "called," Acts 26:15-18; "separated"—selected at birth, Gal. 1:15. Now Paul is introduced.

b. The gospel, 2-6. It is marked by: (1) *Promise,* see Gen. 3:15; 12:3; Isa. 7:14. (2) *Person:* His deity—"Son of God," proved by His resurrection; His humanity—"Of David," cp. Matt. 1:1; Luke 3:23-31; His character—"spirit of holiness," cp. John 8:46; 16:10. (3) *Paul's apostleship*—a matter of divine "grace," favor, unto "obedience of faith" including "all the nations" and "ye also."

c. The persons addressed, 7. They are residents of Rome; crowned with the love of God; who in character are "saints," holy ones; and are recipients of divine favor and peace.

2. Personal interest, 8-15. Several matters disclose Paul's interest in the brethren.

a. His thanksgiving to God for their fame in the faith, 8. Turning from idols to the living God could not fail to be talked about. Here is a famous church, cp. 16:19. Why thank God through Jesus Christ? Col. 3:17; I Tim. 2:5.

b. His prayer in their behalf, 9, 10. It is that God may open a way for him to visit them. The petition is indeed sincere, constant and attested by God.

c. His longing to see them, 11-13. Three reasons assigned:

Impartation of spiritual gifts, see I Cor. 12:4-11; mutual comfort—the gospel effect on them would react on Paul, some fruit among them also. How hindered? 15:21, 22.

d. His spiritual indebtedness to all men, 14, 15. Why a debtor? See Acts 26:16-18. cp. Mark 16:15. Why want to preach at Rome? (1) Because of need. Lightfoot speaks of Rome as "the common sink of all the worst vices of humanity." (2) Because of vantage. Here all commerce met and all religions were exhibited. Pliny, born about A.D. 61, says: "In Rome the gods of the whole world could be examined."

PART I.
SALVATION BY FAITH IN AND OBEDIENCE TO CHRIST, 1:16—11:36.

I. THE PROPOSITION: SALVATION BY THE GOSPEL FOR JEWS AND GENTILES, 1:16, 17.

Paul is ready to preach the gospel for two reasons: he is in debt and wants to pay, 14; he is not ashamed of the gospel, see Acts 28:22; I Cor. 1:23.

Distinctive characteristics of the gospel:

a. It is *"power."* Only divine power can turn man from Satan to God.

b. It is *"unto salvation."* Salvation from verb meaning to restore to health, to heal. Man is spiritually sick; Christ is the physician, Matt. 9:12; the gospel is His prescription.

c. It is *"for everyone."* No racial distinction. Recall Jewish and Gentile prejudice, note Matt. 28:19.

d. It is *conditional.* "Everyone that believeth," but not faith only, 16:26.

e. It reveals *"righteousness."* A God kind of righteousness, hence a perfect system of religion and morality for all time and place.

This righteousness results "from faith," without which no one comes to God, Heb. 11:16; and, since it is revealed, that revelation is "unto faith," Rom. 10:17. Thus the righteous "live by faith."

II. THE PROPOSITION DEFENDED, 1:18—3:20.

1. Failure of the Gentiles, 1:18-32.

a. Knowledge of God from tradition and nature deserted for idolatry, 18-23. Here is inspired history of origin of false religion. It was occasioned by refusal of divine revelation, vain reasoning, image worship.

b. Judicial abandonment to abominable sins, 24-32. Here is a view of people without the Bible and God. These characteristics were derived from the gods worshiped and there were no public laws prohibiting them.

2. Failure of the Jews, 2:1—3:8.

a. Self-delusion in merely possessing the law without doing it, 2:1-16. This also finds practice in Christianity today.

They practiced the same things they condemned in the Gentiles, 1-3. cp. Matt. 7:1-3.

Deeds will determine the judgment to come, 4-11, cp. Matt. 25:31-46.

Standards to be used at the judgment, 12-16. They will be: the law of Moses for the Jews while under that law; the law of conscience for the unevangelized; the gospel for the evangelized. See John 12:48.

b. The Jews openly exposed and condemned, 2:17-29. The searching question to doctors and scribes of the law was, why "teachest thou not thyself?" A case of "Do as I tell you, not as I do." The flagrant conduct described caused the name of God to be blasphemed among the Gentiles. Circumcision was of no value without keeping the law. The Gentiles without circumcision, who lived the spirit of the law, stood a better chance of salvation than the circumcised Jews whose only hope lay in the circumcision of the heart. Note Matt. 15:19. True religion is not formal and outward but spiritual and inward.

c. Jewish objections stated and answered, 3:1-8. The Jews held they were God's chosen people, hence should be favored above Gentiles. But Paul, in chaps. 1, 2, has shown that Jews are no better than Gentiles; both have held down the truth by their wicked lives and are lost. Now a dialogue between the Jews and Paul follows.

The Jew, vs. 1. From preceding reasoning, what advantage

have the Jews over the Gentiles? The answer would seem "none."

Paul, vs. 2. "Much," in particular they possessed the oracles of God. See Ps. 147:19, 20.

The Jew, vs. 3. What about the covenant-keeping God, if He cuts us off from the blessings promised?

Paul, vs. 4. These promises are conditional, see Deut. 28:1-19. Since the Jews failed to live the covenant, God is still truthful if He rejects them.

The Jew, vs. 5. If our unrighteousness advertises God's justice by punishing us when we go wrong, is He not unjust in imposing eternal punishment?

Paul, vss. 6-8. No, for (1) if sin ceases to be sin, how shall God judge the world? And (2) why don't you cease persecuting me? If your reasoning is correct, why may I not say (as I am slanderously reported), "Let us do evil that good may come."

3. Restatement of the fact that the whole world is guilty and under the judgment of God, 3:9-20. "We," Jews, are no better than "they," Gentiles. The indictment describes (a) the state of sin, 10-12; (b) the practice of sin, 13-17. The cause of it all is named in 18, and the law has no remedy, 19, 20.

It is now observed that *before* conversion there is no difference between Jews and Gentiles—both have sinned. Moreover, both have equal rights in the gospel, for both need it in order to be saved. That should remove prejudice among them.

III. THE PROPOSITION EXPOUNDED, 3:21-5:21.

1. The gospel method of justification explained, 3:21-31. Here is the greatest, most complete summary of the Christian doctrine found in the New Testament.

Subject: *"Righteousness of God."*

a. Marks a new epoch—"now," 21, cp. Gal. 4:4.

b. Is independent of the law, 21, cp. Rom. 10:4.

c. Witnessed by the law and the prophets, 21, cp. Matt. 5:17.

d. Experienced through faith in Jesus Christ, 22, cp. Rom. 10:17.

e. Necessary for Jews and Gentiles, "no distinction," 22, 23, cp. Eph. 2:14.

f. Has come through grace, 24, cp. Eph. 2:8.

g. Depends on Jesus as a ransom, 24, 25. By Him we are "justified" (made guiltless), have "redemption" (release from penalty and guilt of sin), "propitiation" (covering of sin).

h. Demonstrates God to be just and justifier, 26. This by providing a victim demanded by His law, Ezek. 18:4; II Cor. 5:14, and cleansing from sin by blood of Christ, vs. 25, I John 1:7.

i. Excludes boasting of Jews and Gentiles, 27-30. Both are saved as pardoned criminals; God is impartial.

j. Confirms the law, 31. It offers no remedy for sin, vs. 20, but Christ does, hence no conflict between law and gospel.

2. The gospel method of justification illustrated and applied, 4:1-25. Having shown in chap. 3 that salvation is obtained only through faith in Christ, the argument is now driven home by the best personal example to the Jews.

a. Abraham was not justified by works, but by faith and divine favor, 1-6; "According to the flesh" Abraham believed God's promise of a numerous posterity, Gen. 15:5, 6; no work of any kind was required, only faith in God's word. Likewise through faith God "justifieth the ungodly."

b. David also speaks of righteousness without works, 6-8. Thus justification by faith is attested by two greatest men the Jews ever had.

c. Abraham not justified by circumcision, 9-12. Righteousness by faith is for everybody, without circumcision, for it was reckoned to Abraham long before he was circumcised. Circumcision was "a sign" or mark indicating that Abraham and his descendants were Jehovah's chosen people. It was also "a seal," or God's approval of Abraham's faith, a model for all believers in Christ.

d. Abraham and his seed not heirs by means of the law, but by faith, 13-25.

(1) The world inheritance is based on faith, 13-17, cp. Gen. 17:4-6; 22:17, 18. Note I John 5:1, 4, 5.

(2) The strength of Abraham's faith, 18-22. The kind of faith required then and now is that which does not doubt God's word, no more, no less. This is saving faith.

(3) Abraham a type of all believers in Christ, 23-25. They must believe two facts concerning Christ: first His death for

our sins, see I Pet. 2:24; second, His resurrection for our justification—acquittal. In heaven He applies His blood to the sinner, Heb. 9:12, 24.

Summary of Abraham's Faith in Chapter 4

1. It was based on God's word.
2. Placed him among the righteous.
3. Was approved by "sign" and "seal."
4. Made him a father of all believers.
5. Enabled him and his seed to inherit the world through Christ.
6. Is required of all men now.

In this short chapter Paul tells us more about faith than do all the writings of theologians.

3. Results of justification by faith in Christ, 5:1-5. They are:

"Peace" through reconciliation, II Cor. 5:18.

"Access" to divine favor, Eph. 1:3.

Joy—we "rejoice" (a) in sharing God's glory, Phil. 3:20, 21; (b) in tribulation, for it results in "steadfastness, approvedness, hope." See James 1:12.

"The Love of God" imparted by the Holy Spirit, note Acts 2:38; 5:32.

4. Description of our state of condemnation, 5:6-11. We were:

"Weak," unable to save ourselves. Recall Gentiles and Jews, chaps. 1, 2.

"Ungodly": ignored God and His book.

"Sinners": (a) transgressed God's law, I John 3:4; (b) refused to repent though God was good, Rom. 2:4.

"Enemies" despite God's love in Christ, cp. John 3:16.

5. The great value of Christ in contrast with Adam, 5:12-21.

How did sin enter the world? 12. Adam and Eve heard, believed and obeyed a lie, Gen. 3:1-5, the effect of which was death, 2:16, 17.

How did all men sin in Adam? Not volitionally, because not yet born. But Adam and Eve transmitted to posterity a *tendency* to sin. Note Gen. 5:3; Ps. 51:5. And people do sin.

What proof that all men share in Adam's penalty? 13, 14. They die. This is inevitable, because Adam and descendants were cut off from the tree of life, Gen. 3:22, 23.

What are the points of comparison between Adam and Christ? 15-17.

(a) Adam caused death; Christ nullifies death by resurrection, 15.

(b) Adam caused "condemnation"; Christ provides "justification," or acquittal, 16.

(c) Adam caused reign of death; Christ offers joint-rule with Him in life, 17.

The conclusion, 18-21, a recapitulation from vs. 12 onward. (a) By one sin all men have been condemned to death, likewise by one act of righteousness (Christ's death) all may have life. (b) By Adam's disobedience all were constituted sinners; by Christ's obedience (Phil. 2:8) all may be constituted righteous. (c) The law, by its many restrictions, increased the sin (cp. 7:7) resulting in a reign of death; grace superabounded, effecting a reign unto eternal life—the sensational good news through Jesus Christ.

IV. THE OBJECTIONS OF THE JEWS STATED AND MET, 6:1—7:25.

1. Objection concerning abundance of grace, 6:1-14.

a. Objection stated, see 5:20. 1: "Let us commit more sin so as to have more grace."

b. Reply, 2-14; No, because—

(1) We died to sin through union with Christ in baptism, 2-11. In baptism is:

A death to sin. We "died to sin," 2, when "baptized into his death," 3, "crucified with him," 6. And as He "died unto sin once," 10, so do we in baptism; from then on we must remain "dead unto sin," 11.

A burial, 4. Christ "bore our sins in his body upon the tree," I Pet. 2:24; cp. II Cor. 5:21. Like as His body of sin was buried, so our "old man," "the body of sin," 6, was buried out of sight forever. Only immersion in water is burial.

A resurrection. "Like as Christ was raised" to a new life with God, so we are raised from the watery grave to "walk in newness of life," 4, "the likeness of his resurrection" life, 5. Hence, "to me to live is Christ," Phil. 1:21.

(2) The conclusion, 12-14. We are to live a life of righteous-

ness. Not sin, but God must have dominion, 12, 13. This we can do, for we are not under the law, which has no mercy nor means of forgiveness, 14.

2. Objection concerning freedom from the law, 6:15—7:6.

a. The objection stated, 15, recall 14: "Since we are not under the law which points out sin, let us sin."

b. Reply, 6:16—7:6: No, because—

(1) As slaves we have a new master, 6:16-23. Change from master sin to master righteousness is effected by obedience to "form [*typon* = mould, imprint, pattern] of teaching." The sinner is put into the gospel mould and comes out a Christian free from sin, 15-18.

The new life is totally different from the old of which we are now "ashamed" and it ends in spiritual "death"; the new is "unto sanctification" and ends in "eternal life," a gift bestowed *"in* Christ."

(2) As a wife we have a new husband, 7:1-6. In 6:14 onward it is reasoned a Christian may not sin though he is not under the law which points out sin. Now Paul shows *how* one is released from the law, illustrating it by the law of marriage. Two points are made:

(a) The law of wedlock is dissolved only by death, 1-3. If, while both parties live, the wife marries another man, she is stigmatized an adulteress; but if death has intervened she may remarry.

(b) Remarriage to Christ, 4-6. This is permissible because "ye were made dead to the law," our former husband. But how?

(1) We by human nature were in Christ, Phil. 2:7, our representative in death, II Cor. 5:14, 15.

(2) Christ was born, lived and died under the law of Moses. Therefore, when He died we died to the law through Him, being "crucified with him" 6:6. But He "was raised from the dead," and now we are "joined," "espoused" (II Cor. 11:2), to Him.

Thus sin by the instrument of the law has no power over us.

3. Objection to the law with reference to sin, 7:7-12.

a. The objection stated, 7a: "Since blessings follow release from the law, it must be sin."

b. Reply, 7b-12: No, because—

(1) Knowledge of sin comes through the law, 7. Its "Thou

shalt nots" cover the whole range of sin. It was needed before salvation could be wanted or appreciated.

(2) Sin through the law caused me to desire things forbidden by the law, 7, 8. "Apart from the law sin is dead." Cp. I John 3:4.

(3) Sin through the law slew me, 9-11: Therefore "the power of sin is the law," I Cor. 15:56.

(4) Hence the law is not evil, but holy, righteous and good, 12.

4. Objection to the law in regard to death, 7:13-25.

a. The objection stated, 13: "Since the law involves man in death, it must be the cause of death."

b. Reply, 14-25: No, for—

(1) Sin, through the law, is the cause of death, 13. Sin is exceeding sinful in that it works evil by that which is good.

(2) The law is spiritual, but I am carnal, 14-24. Here is a fierce battle between the "flesh" with its appetites and passions and "the inward man" or spirit. It is *war against the soul,"* I Pet. 2:11. My purpose is to do right, but sin makes me fail. It appears this was Paul's struggle with sin before his conversion— a hopeless battle under the law.

(3) Victory through Christ, 25. Though not under the law, Christians experience the same struggle between flesh and spirit, but with this difference: they are "more than conquerors" (Rom. 8:37) through Jesus Christ.

V. COMPLETE REDEMPTION THROUGH CHRIST, 8:1-39.

This chapter follows the shout of victory in 7:25 and is the climax of the epistle.

1. Freedom in the gospel from all condemnation, 1-11.

a. The fact stated, 1-4. In Christ is no condemnation, for the law of the Spirit, the gospel, liberates—a thing the law of Moses could not do, 3:20. This freedom was procured by Christ, who met sin in its citadel, "the flesh," where it was defeated by His sinless life and atoning death. Thus as our representative He by perfect obedience fulfilled the ordinance of the law in which we had failed.

b. The contrast, 4-11.

(1) Those governed by the flesh, 5-8. What is wrong? The *intellect*—"mind of the flesh"; the *affections*—"enmity against

God"; the *will*—"not subject to the law of God"; the *life*—"cannot please God." How changed? See gospel plan of salvation.

(2) Those governed by the Spirit, 9-11. God and Christ dwell in them through the Holy Spirit, John 14:16, 17, 23. That ends sin and assures the resurrection.

2. Obligation and possibility of living in Christ, 12-17. To the flesh we owe nothing, only to the Spirit, who by His indwelling and word enables us against the flesh (see Acts 2:38; Gal. 5:16, 18, 25), and testifies "we are children of God" and "heirs" if we suffer.

3. Encouragement to endure suffering, 18-39.

a. The hope of the resurrection, 18-25. After suffering will be glory, illustrated by "creation" personified. It was subjected to "vanity," "pain," by the curse, Gen. 3:17, 18, but is looking forward to release (see II Pet. 3:13; Rev. 21:1, 5). Likewise we suffer in many ways and "groan," waiting for "redemption of our body" from the grave.

b. The help of the Holy Spirit, 26, 27. At times in distress we know not what to pray for, so we groan, prompted by help promised in the Spirit's word. Hence the Spirit is said to intercede with groanings (ours) "according to the will of God" revealed.

c. The fulfillment of the divine purpose, 28-30. In everything God works good to those who love Him. "According to his purpose" as follows. He—

"Foreknew"—chose them in Christ before creation, Eph. 1:4, cp. Acts 10:34, 35.

"Foreordained"—to be like Christ, Gal. 4:19. Note: Foreordination here concerns groups, "them," not individuals. Is based on man's attitude toward Christ, Acts 13:48. Here "foreordained" means disposed, cp. vs. 45.

"Called"—through the gospel, II Thess. 2:13, 14.

"Justified"—meaning: (1) to make one guiltless, (2) to declare one guiltless, hence, to acquit.

"Glorified"—in the resurrection, Phil. 3:20, 21.

d. The security of God's elect, 31-39. God backs His people. No one, like accuser in court, can bring a charge. If the Judge acquits the case is ended.

Christ backs His people. They are His by purchase, I Cor. 6:20.

"Who shall separate us?" Only *we* can do it.

Therefore eternal security depends on three parties: "God," 31; "Christ," 34; "we," 37. "Once in grace, always in grace" is not in the New Testament.

VI. JUSTIFICATION BY FAITH RECONCILED WITH GOD'S REJECTION OF ISRAEL, 9:1—11:36.

1. Paul's interest in his own nation, 9:1-5. His sorrow for them, expressed in willing self-sacrifice, was deeply felt because of their rejection despite so many privileges and honors.

2. Ground on which *God* is justified in rejecting Israel, 9:6-29. The Jews raise objections and Paul replies.

a. First objection, 6-13: "The word of God has failed, because as children of Abraham they should all be accepted."

Reply: No, God's word has not failed, for—

(1) The twelve tribes do not constitute all Israel, 6. There is spiritual Israel, 2:28, 29, descendants of Abraham, 4:11-13.

(2) A descendant of Abraham does not necessarily make one acceptable to God, 7-9. "In Isaac shall thy seed be called" (chosen), hence Ishmael was excluded.

(3) Moreover, God's promise left Him free to use His will in regard to His purpose, 10-13. Jacob was better fitted for that purpose than was Esau, hence chosen.

From all this it appears that God is not inconsistent with His promise to Abraham.

b. Second objection, 14-18: "God is unrighteous in use of His power, as seen in that He preferred Isaac to Ishmael and Jacob to Esau."

Reply. No, for—

(1) He has mercy on whom He pleases, 14-16. Abraham *willed* that Ishmael should be chosen, Gen. 17:18, but God said Isaac, Gen. 21:11, 12. Esau *ran* for venison, Gen. 27:1-4, but God wanted it otherwise. His mercy is seen in His choice of fit men for His purpose, for it was a purpose of mercy.

(2) He hardens whom He pleases, 17, 18. Pharaoh was permitted to go on in rebellion until he was past feeling, Ex. 8:15, 32; cp. 9:12; 10:20. It was Pharaoh's *will* against God's *word* which resulted in a hard heart. Likewise God permits the Jews

to reject their Messiah, but "their minds were hardened," II Cor. 3:14, just like Pharaoh's heart.

c. Third objection, 19-29: "From the above it appears God has acted arbitrarily, hence who can help himself?"

Reply:

(1) Reproof, 20, 21.

(2) The Jews and others fitted themselves either for destruction or salvation, cp. Acts 13:45, 48. On potter and clay see Jer. 18:1-10.

(3) Rejection of Israel and choice of Gentiles foretold by Hosea, hence ought not to surprise the Jews, 25, 26.

(4) The reason for Israel's rejection was their wickedness, according to Isaiah, 27-29.

d. Conclusion as to why God rejected Israel, 30-33:

(1) The blessing promised to Abraham was obtained by the Gentiles through faith, 30. Therefore God's promise has not failed because they were included in it, Gen. 12:3.

(2) The Jews lost the blessing because they sought it by *works* instead of by *faith,* 31, 32.

(3) This was predicted by Isaiah, 33. God had forewarned them, hence not blamable.

3. Ground on which *Israel* was rejected, 10:1-21. In chap. 9 *God* is fully vindicated, now *Israel* goes on trial.

a. They sought righteousness by the law instead of by faith in Christ, 1-5. However, their condition could be changed, for Paul prayed for them; they were ignorant concerning Christ and the law.

b. Righteousness by faith explained, 6-15. Personified, righteousness says:

(1) It is not hard to obtain, 6-8. Negatively, do not demand re-enactment of Christ's coming and resurrection in order to believe. Those are attested historical facts. Positively, it is near you in the word of faith proclaimed.

(2) It consists of faith in and confession of Christ, 9, 10. Cp. Matt. 16:16; 10:32. These are conditions of salvation but not the only ones, Acts 2:38.

(3) It is offered to all who call upon the name of the Lord, 11-13. No distinction—"all have sinned," 3:23; all have the same Lord.

(4) How to call upon the name of the Lord, 14, 15. The requisites are believing, hearing, preacher, sending. Without these *it can't be done.*

c. Israel's failure stated and exposed, 16-21. There is no excuse for unbelief because—

(1) Faith rests upon testimony, 16, 17. This they refused to believe; nevertheless, faith comes by hearing the word.

(2) All have heard and could understand, 18-21. The Gentiles—"them that sought me not"—responded, but Israel was "a disobedient and gainsaying people."

4. Israel's rejection neither total nor final, 11:1-32.

a. Not total, because only a part of Israel had been hardened, 1-10. No, God did not cast off all His people. Paul and other believers, called "a remnant," prove exception. To suppose all are rejected is to repeat the error of Elijah.

"Hardened" was the reason for rejection, hence "God gave them a spirit of stupor," like an anesthesia. Spiritually this affected their *"eyes"*—they will not look at Jesus as their Messiah, John 19:15; *"ears"*—they will not hear the gospel, cp. Matt. 13:14, 15; *"table"*—they sit at Moses' table instead of Christ's, John 9:28; 6:35; *"back"*—they are in political and spiritual slavery, John 8:34, 32. This is the present terrible status of the Jews, but there is hope.

b. Not final, because of equal opportunity with the Gentiles, 11-32. No, they fell not without recovery. However, "by their fall salvation came to the Gentiles," 11, Acts 13:46.

And if their fall enriched the world (Gentiles), much more will their "fulness" (conversion) result in "life from the dead" among Gentiles by their evangelistic zeal, 12-15.

Moreover, if some of them have been accepted, so will the rest, 16.

Gentiles are warned against pride and unbelief lest they also be rejected, 17-22.

The Jews may come back "if they continue not in their unbelief," 23, 24.

Information concerning Israel's salvation, 25-32. Summarily stated, it will be:

1. By means of the gospel, 1:16.
2. On condition of faith, 11:23.

3. When "the fulness" (full number of the Gentiles) comes into the church, 25. "So," in this order, will their Deliverer come, who has already gone forth from Zion, 26, see Luke 24:47; Acts 2.

4. According to covenant, 27. It states terms of salvation. Cp. Jer. 31:31-34.

As Gentiles were disobedient, 1:18-32, yet obtained mercy, so the same mercy is extended to Jews, 28-32.

5. Conclusion from the whole argument, 33-36: So vast and inscrutable is the divine plan of salvation that only God could devise it and only the inspired Apostle could trace it.

At close of 3:20, it was observed that there was no difference between Jews and Gentiles *before* conversion—both needed salvation. Now Paul has shown that *in* conversion there was no difference between them—both became Christians in the same way, hence should live together in peace.

PART II.
PRACTICAL, HORTATORY AND CONCLUSION, 12:1—16:27.

Having demonstrated by Scriptures and keen logic what righteousness by faith is, the Apostle now applies the teaching to life in the church.

I. DUTIES TO GOD AND MEN, 12:1—15:13.

1. Complete devotion to God, 12:1, 2. The appeal is based on "mercies" of God; calls for a life of sacrificial "service" (marg., "worship"), hence daily living is worshiping God; accomplished by one "transformed"—moulded by the gospel, 6:17; the design is to "prove" to the world the will of God, Matt. 5:16.

2. Duties to those within the church, 12:3-16.

a. Special duties. They are (1) humility, 3; (2) co-operative service based on "gifts"—spiritual and natural endowments, 4-8.

b. General duties, 9-16. The basic element for all these virtues is "love" for God and men. Note John 14:23.

3. Duties to those outside the church, 12:17-21. The Christian lives in a world of "evil" people. The only way to win against

them is by the "good"—one means by which Satan is defeated. Example, II Kings 6:8-23.

4. Duties to civil authority, 13:1-7. The church with Christ as head was established within a pagan empire. What should be her conduct toward the state? That dilemma demands divine wisdom then and now.

Reasons for subjection and support, 1-7:

a. *"God."* All authority is from Him. He rules non-Christians through civil authority, the Christian through Christ.

b. *"Rulers."* They are protection against evildoers, hence to be obeyed, except un-Christian demands.

c. *"Conscience,"* because the state is of God, note I Pet. 2:13.

d. *"Dues."* "Tribute"—taxes; "custom"—tariff; "fear"—obedience; "honor"—respect. Without these civil government could not operate.

5. The duty of love to all men, 8-10. "Owe no man" any of the above dues; if private debts are contracted, pay them; the debt of love is never paid in full.

6. All these duties enforced by consideration that salvation is near, 11-14. Salvation into the eternal kingdom, II Pet. 1:11, draws nearer each day. Therefore let the Christian: (a) *wake up:* "day is at hand," cp. Eph. 5:14; (b) *dress up:* "put on the armor," cp. Eph. 6:11, 12; (c) *go to work:* "walk becomingly," cp. Phil. 2:12.

7. Christian conduct by the strong and the weak in the faith, 14:1—15:13. In 13:14 it reads: "put ye on (as a garment) the Lord Jesus Christ." He puts limitations on the flesh and also solves difficulties discussed in chap. 14 onward.

a. Mutual forbearance in matters of opinion, 14:1-23. In summary the governing principles are:

(1) In opinion, liberty, 1. In the church were Jews and Gentiles having opinions about meats, drinks and special days. These opinions they tried to enforce on each other. But in these matters neither was to judge the other, for judgment belongs to God.

(2) Conduct according to conscience, 5, 14, 20. Rule is: Never do anything not approved by conscience. It is the moral executive of the soul.

(3) Peace and edification of the church, 19. It is the body of

Christ and should be edified (built up), not destroyed by contentions.

An axiom for our day: "All within the Bible is faith; all outside the Bible is opinion."

b. Obligation of the strong to the weak, 15:1-13. Subject matter in chap. 14 is continued. Strength should serve weakness, for "none liveth to himself," 14:7, illustrated by example of Christ and enforced by Scriptures, 1-6.

Motive for Jews and Gentiles to receive each other is "the glory of God," 7-13. (1) The Jews should glorify Him for His *truth*, because the Christ confirmed God's promises to the fathers, 8. (2) The Gentiles should glorify Him for His *mercy*, predicted in Old Testament Scriptures.

We now pause for summary of reasons why Jews and Gentiles should live in harmony in the church. First, *before* conversion there was no difference between them—both were in sin and in need of salvation. Second, *in* conversion there was no difference, for both parties were saved by faith in Christ and obedience to Him. Finally, *after* conversion they should "receive one another" even as Christ had received them, and so live in peace. These reasons are just as valid in the church now as then.

II. CONCLUSION, 15:14—16:27.

1. Personal matters, 15:14-33.

a. Paul's confidence in the brethren, 14. This was said to secure action in regard to his teaching.

b. Reasons for writing so boldly, 15, 16. This he could do because of "grace" of apostleship which qualified and authorized him to teach them.

c. His labors as an apostle, 17-21. Humbly he could boast:

(1) In what Christ had done through him, 17-19.

(2) In preaching where Christ was not known, 20, 21.

d. His purpose to visit them, 22-29. The time is set by two events:

(1) When he goes to Spain. That would give occasion for fellowship with the brethren and assistance from them.

(2) After he has taken the offering to Jerusalem. This offering, for the poor saints in Judea, Paul had called for from churches in Macedonia, Achaia and Galatia, cp. I Cor. 16:1-3.

e. His request for their prayers, 30-33. They were to pray:

(1) That he may be delivered from the unbelieving Jews in Judea. He saw the storm gathering against him.

(2) That the believing Jews may accept the offering. Racial prejudice was strong.

2. Commendation, greetings, warning and benediction, 16:1-27.

a. Commendation and salutation, 1-16. Phoebe, the probable bearer of the letter, is commended for her helpfulness.

Salutation from Paul is directed to a large number of men and women in the church because of distinguished character and service, closing with greetings from "all the churches of Christ." Here is revealed character study, and a generous spirit of praise often neglected in the church now.

b. Warning against division makers, 17-20. Jewish zealots for the law and pagan philosophers made it necessary for the church to be on guard. Her duty was to *"mark,"* meaning to observe attentively, carefully; and to *"turn away,"* have no fellowship with division makers. They serve not the Lord, but their own stomachs—bread and butter preachers. Paul was confident the church would act, for her obedience is "come abroad," thus "the God of peace" would bruise Satan, the instigator of divisions. Here is program for Christian unity.

c. Salutation of Paul's companions, 21-24. They were Paul's evangelistic committee in Corinth, whence the letter was sent. He seldom worked alone.

d. Benediction, 25-27. Paul's desire for the church was that God may *"establish,"* put her on a solid base:

(1) "According to my gospel," proclaiming Jesus Christ, nothing else.

(2) "According to revelation." The "mystery" of past ages, but now revealed, was "Christ the hope of glory," Col. 1:27. All mystery is revealed by the gospel.

(3) "According to the commandment." The eternal God has ordered preaching of the gospel "unto all the nations unto obedience of faith," Mark 16:15. This is the one business of the church to the glory of God through Jesus Christ the mediator. "Amen."

First Letter to Corinth

INTRODUCTION.

1. Corinth the city. It was famous for wealth, vice and culture. "To live as they do in Corinth" was a proverbial saying of the times and meant luxury and licentiousness. Strabo tells us that in the temple of Venus "there were more than a thousand harlots," dedicated to the queen of love. Its educational and commercial life is indicated by Cicero, who speaks of it as "the light of all Greece," and by Florus, who describes it as "the ornament of Greece."

2. Establishing the church, Acts 18. In it were some Jews of note, vs. 8, but the majority were Gentiles, I Cor. 12:2.

3. Place and time of writing. The letter was written at Ephesus in A.D. 57, during Paul's third missionary tour (54-58), deduced from I Cor. 16:8, 19; Acts 18:18, 19. That Paul had written them a letter before this, now lost, is evident from I Cor. 5:9.

4. Occasion. It was written to correct certain sins and disorders in the church named in the letter. It serves, therefore, as *a manual with reference to church problems,* hence of inestimable value to the church now.

ANALYSIS AND NOTES

INTRODUCTION, 1:1-9.

1. The writer, 1. His office is stated; some in the church denied his apostleship, 9:1; II Cor. 12:12.

2. The persons addressed, 2, 3. "Church of God"—planner; "sanctified"—made holy, set apart for holy service; "called"—

27

through the gospel, II Thess. 2:14; "with all...in every place" —you and me included.

3. Gifts of God in Christ, 4-9. "Utterance," "knowledge"— endowed with tongues to speak and what to say, see 12:8-10; "Come behind in no gift"—had same gifts as all other churches. Thus "the testimony of Christ was confirmed" to all in fellowship with Him.

PART I.
DIVISION AND CONTENTION IN THE CHURCH
1:10—4:21.

I. THE WAY TO UNITY AND PEACE, 1:10-17.

1. The authoritative name, 10a. "All authority" is vested in Jesus Christ, Matt. 28:18; His name "is above every name," Phil. 2:9; therefore He only is to be heard on all church problems, Matt. 17:5.

2. The human possibility, 10b, 11.

Of speech—"speak the same," namely "the oracles of God," I Pet. 4:11. The Bible does not divide people, only human opinions.

Of organization—"no divisions." Solved by divine "pattern" for the church, Heb. 8:5.

Of mind—the mind of Christ, Phil. 2:5. Thus can think alike.

Of judgment— word means resolve, purpose; hence unity consummated by act of will.

Thus "contentions" are eliminated.

3. The divine imperative, 12-17.

a. The one Christ. The church is His body, Eph. 1:22, 23; different parties represent a divided Christ; hence there must be organic unity—"one flock, one shepherd," John 10:16.

b. The death of Christ. "He died for all," II Cor. 5:15; therefore the one atonement demands unity among Christians.

c. Baptism into the name of Christ. His name is received in baptism, Acts 19:5; human names are divisive, vs. 12; therefore unity is obtained in His name only.

II. "THE WORD OF THE CROSS" COMPARED WITH "THE WISDOM OF THE WORLD," 1:18–2:16.

1. The word of the cross declared "foolishness," 1:18. Is thus spoken of by "them that perish," being wise in their own conceit.

2. The so-called "foolishness of God" vindicated, 1:19-31.

a. By prophecy, 19. Overthrow of human wisdom is predicted.

b. By preaching the gospel, 20, 21. Human wisdom is exposed by ignorance of God and failure to save men, but the gospel brought results.

c. By the person of Christ, 22-25. He is the wisdom of God revealed, Matt. 11:27; the power of God to save, Acts 4:12.

d. By personnel of the church in Corinth, 26-31. This proves the church there was not due to worldly wisdom but to the gospel of Christ.

3. "The testimony of God" versus philosophy and oratory, 2:1–8.

a. Paul's preaching, 1-5. Not flowery speech and earthly wisdom but Christ and Him crucified, demonstrated by miracles. Thus faith rests in *power* of God.

b. The utter failure of worldly wisdom, 6-8. Seen in:

(1) The spiritual size of Corinthians, 6. Worldly wisdom failed to make them grow; they were spiritual runts.

(2) The ignorant conduct of rulers toward Jesus, 7, 8. See Luke 23:34.

4. The wisdom of God, 2:9-16.

a. Revealed by the Spirit, 9-13. God's blessings for His children are beyond human discovery but known by the Holy Spirit, who inspired the apostles as to "things" and "words." Note Matt. 10:19, 20.

b. Understood by the man of the Spirit, 14-16. "The natural man" represents, not the unconverted man, as held by some, but false teachers in the church who have caused divisions. He is a psychical man, *one governed entirely by the senses,* as were the Greek philosophers. To such the gospel was "foolishness." But "he that is spiritual," *one endowed by the Holy Spirit,* like the apostles, vs. 13, "judgeth [examines] all things"; is instructed by nobody, for he has "the mind of Christ"—superhuman thinking.

III. THE CORRECT CONCEPTION OF AND ATTITUDE TOWARD THE CHURCH OF CHRIST, 3:1–4:21.

1. Its workers with God, 3:1-9.

a. Paul's adaptation of teaching to the Corinthians, 1-4. They were babes who must have "milk," not "meat." Such they were when he left them five or six years before, and also when he wrote, evidenced by their party spirit; hence he must adapt his teaching to their condition. "Carnal" means "having the nature of flesh"—self-pleasing, the essence of sectarianism.

b. Apostles and associates are "ministers" (servants), not party leaders, 5-9. As such, Paul planted the church by preaching, Apollos through his eloquence (Acts 18:24) watered it by teaching. God made them grow. Thus figuratively the church was God's farm and building.

2. Its foundation and superstructure, 3:10-15. For this "building," 9, Paul laid foundation by preaching Christ, cp. 2:2; Eph. 2:20. Two kinds of material used in Corinth for superstructure: one is fireproof—gospel teaching and living; the other is combustible—false teaching and living; both tested by the judgment day.

3. Its sacredness and care, 3:16, 17. "Temple" means inner shrine like Holy of holies in Jewish Tabernacle where God dwelt. The Christian is raised to the lights of heaven. The church is destroyed by false teaching and wicked members.

4. Its attitude toward human wisdom in spiritual things, 3:18-23. Such wisdom is deceptive, foolishness with God and vain. Hence boast not in men, for all things are yours in Christ—boundless wealth!

5. Its apostles and evangelists, 4:1-21.

a. Their office and responsibility, 1-5. As "ministers" they are subject to Christ; as "stewards" they provide for God's household; as responsibles the Lord is their Judge.

b. Their contrast with disturbers in Corinth, 6-13. Kindness caused Paul and Apollos to be scapegoats for wrong of favorite teachers. All good in the church had come only from Paul and associates, who suffered much from hardships and slander.

c. Fatherly admonition and counsel, 14-21. Though many teachers, yet one spiritual father: Paul begat them through the gospel. See James 1:18; I Pet. 1:23. Therefore imitate him and heed his warning.

PART II.
REPLIES TO REPORTS AND QUESTIONS
5:1—11:16.

I. REPORT CONCERNING INCEST, 5:1-13.

1. Discipline of a fornicator in the church, 1-8. The offense involved stepmother and son, condoned by teachers "puffed up" by pagan philosophy; withdrawal of fellowship was ordered, which might save the man, if he repents, and keep the church from contamination; therefore "purge out the old leaven, . . . let us keep the feast" of clean living, see Ex. 12:15-20.

2. Explanation of a misunderstood passage in a former letter, 9-13. "No company" did not include outsiders, only criminals in the church; therefore "put away the wicked man."

II. REPORT CONCERNING LAWSUITS AND ABUSE OF CHRISTIAN LIBERTY, 6:1-20.

1. Differences between Christians to be settled within the church, 1-6. Lawsuits among Christians declared wrong for these reasons: (a) The wrong tribunal. Pagan courts then, civil courts now, could not render Christian verdict according to human law. (b) Saints are to judge the world and angels. In Matt. 25:40, 41, Christ is identified with His people at the judgment, hence it seems they shall act through Him. (c) It degrades the church: is there not "among you one wise man?"

2. Wickedness of lawsuits exposed and condemned, 7-11. By court action it was planned beforehand to defraud. Instead, why not suffer wrong? "Be not deceived"—the kingdom of God is not for the wicked, only for the "washed," "sanctified," "justified."

3. Christian liberty misapplied and corrected, 12-20. Gratify every desire was the teaching of Epicurean philosophy.

In 12, 13a, is a two-way conversation in regard to "meats." Unbridled use of meats and drinks is slavery.

Verses 13b-20 contain argument against "fornication." In

temple of Venus were a thousand harlots serving in name of religion. Though somewhat involved, main points are: Christians are members of Christ, hence cannot be joined to a harlot; the body is temple of the Holy Spirit, not for unholy conduct; Christians belong to Christ by purchase, therefore not their own to do as they please.

III. QUESTIONS ON MARRIAGE, 7:1-40.

1. "Is marriage to be desired or avoided by Christians?" 1-9.

Occasion for the question appears to be this: Jews advocated marriage, Gen. 2:18, 24. Among Greeks some followers of philosopher Pythagoras held it inconsistent with purity.

In reply to the question Paul advises against marriage, (a) because of persecution "distress," 26; however, because of prevailing unchastity, (b) let Christians marry.

2. "Is marriage dissoluble?" 10-24.

In reply Paul cites law of Christ, Matt. 5:32. This applies when both parties are Christians.

In case a couple married in paganism and afterward one became a Christian, separation is allowable—if they cannot live in peace—but re-marriage is prohibited. However, if they can live in peace such wedlock is "sanctified"; there is also possibility of believer saving the unbeliever.

Conclusion is, in some things Christians were to "abide," remain, when called by the gospel.

3. "Is the single life preferable to marriage?" 25-38.

a. Counsel to the unmarried, 25-35. "Virgins" may include both sexes, as in Rev. 14:4; is rendered "unmarried" in R.S.V. Two reasons for the single life: (1) "the distress"—uncertainty of life because of persecution, 26-31. Nero was Caesar. (2) Freedom from care, 32-35. More time for the Lord.

b. Directions to parents, 36-38. Were needed, because it was customary among Jews, Greeks and Romans to give their daughters in marriage.

4. Should widows remarry? 39, 40. They may, "only in the Lord," i. e., to a Christian.

IV. QUESTION CONCERNING IDOLATROUS MEAT, 8:1-13.

Have not Christians liberty to eat meat offered in sacrifice to idols? Reply:

1. Knowledge without love is insufficient, 1-7. "We know," said they. Yes, but some knowledge is conceited, 1; all is imperfect, 2; love is needed, 3. Furthermore, "we know" an idol is nothing, there is but one God, 4-6; but not all believers knew this, so new converts ate sacrifices as offerings to idols, with injury to conscience, 7.

2. Solution of the problem, 8-13. Food is not religion, 8, cp. Rom. 14:17. However, personal liberty must not injure a weak brother, thus sin against Christ, 9-12. The Apostle's resolution, 13.

V. QUESTION CONCERNING PAUL'S MATERIAL SUPPORT, 9:1-27.

"Why, being an apostle, did you not take wages due you?" The false teachers in Corinth wanted support from the church but were hindered by Paul's example of self-support, Acts 18: 1-3; II Cor. 11:7-12. So they denied Paul's apostleship, for if he were an apostle he would have demanded pay.

1. His right to support, 1-14. Made clear as follows:

a. His prerogatives as an apostle, 1-6. As free he was entitled to wages, slaves were not; as an apostle support was due him more than ordinary men; existence of the church in Corinth proved him not an impostor; since the rest of apostles were supported, he had the same right.

b. Arguments proving his right to support, 7-14. Wages are due for service, 7; the law of Moses allows reward for labor, 8-10; the exchange of values, 11; just and impartial treatment, 12; analogy of Jewish priests and Christian teachers, 13; the command of Christ, 14, cp. Matt. 10:10.

2. Why he did not use this right, 15-27. (a) Ground for boasting before the false teachers, 15-18. Paul's superiority to them was in preaching to Corinthians for naught; they wanted pay. (b) Gaining more converts to Christ, 19-23. People could not say he preached for money. (c) Self-control, 24-27. Though

right to support, he restrained himself in order that desires of the flesh might be under control, see Matt. 16:24.

VI. FURTHER REPLY TO QUESTION OF IDOLATROUS MEAT, 10:1—11:1.

Having spoken of self-control at close of chap. 9, Paul resumes discussion of idolatrous meat in chap. 10 and urges complete separation from the old life of sin.

1. Argument by analogy from the history of Israel, 10:1-13. As baptism into Moses in the Red Sea separated Israel from Egyptian bondage, so baptism into Christ draws line between the old life of sin and the new. And as material manna and water became spiritual sustenance because divinely supplied, so material elements of Lord's Supper become spiritual food to Christians, 1-4.

Furthermore, Israel provides type of warning, 5-13. Read events referred to: "idolaters," Ex. 32:1-28; "fornication," Num. 25:1-9; "trial of the Lord," Num. 21:4-6; "murmur," Num. 14:1-3, 29; 16:41-49. "Wherefore...take heed."

2. Sacrificial feasts connect worshiper and object worshiped, 10:14-22. The false teachers held eating in pagan temples meat sacrificed to idols was not idolatry. The error is met by the word "communion," participation: In the Lord's supper, 14-17; in Israel's sacrifices, 18; in pagan feasts, 19-22. Therefore feasting with idolaters in their temples is a moral impossibility.

3. Christian liberty modified by duties to others, 10:23—11:1. Question is whether meat sacrificed to idols might be eaten when sold in the public market. Problem is solved by the word "conscience," that of eater and observer. Rule is: no occasion of stumbling.

VII.   QUESTION CONCERNING HEADDRESS, 11:2-16.

"Ought men to have their heads covered, or may women have their heads uncovered when they pray or prophesy in public?" Reason for question: Jews and Romans worshiped with covered heads, Greeks not.

1. Introductory, 2, 3. A word of praise would secure obedience. Parallels of headship: man over woman, God over Christ.

2. Reasons for uncovering a man's head and covering a woman's head, 4-16.

a. The law of subjection and local custom, 4-6. Covered head a sign of submission, hence to man dishonor; same to woman without veil in the East.

b. The law of creative order and glory, 7-12. Man created first, then woman from man, therefore her veil a sign of man's authority over her. Even angels are under authority, cp. Heb. 1:14. However, man and woman are complementary.

c. The teaching of nature, 13-15. Nature gives man short hair, woman long. Let each sex keep its place. Masculine women and effeminate men are objectionable.

d. The uniform custom of the church, 16. Thus the question is settled without debate.

Note: Paul reasons from local custom and Scriptures. Custom in the East is not enforceable in the West, but Scripture is.

PART III.
CORRECTION OF UNCHRISTIAN CONDUCT AND FALSE TEACHING, 11:17—15:58.

I. DISORDERLY CONDUCT AT THE LORD'S SUPPER, 11:17-34.

1. Factions and intemperance preceding the supper, 17-22. As the Passover preceded institution of the supper, so early Christians observed a "love-feast," Jude 12, preceding the Lord's supper. This was a common meal contributed by all, but in Corinth the poor not able to give were excluded from eating, hence "hungry," while the rich ate and drank to excess. This was divisive. Moreover, groups seem to have formed by factionists (chap. 1). Thus "divisions" existed. Under such condition it was "not possible to eat the Lord's supper," a spiritual fellowship meal, so Paul ordered the love-feast to be eaten at home, for it was no part of the supper.

2. The true nature of the Lord's supper, 23-34. First, the account of its origin, 23-25. This Paul had received from the Lord by inspiration. Next, the spirit and manner of its observance, 26-34. It is a public proclamation, looking backward to the death

of Christ and forward to His return. "Unworthy" is an adverb of conduct, not of character; recall vss. 18-22. Hence let one "prove himself" worthy by conduct at the Lord's table. Failure in this made Corinthians spiritually "weak and sickly."

II. SPIRITUAL GIFTS, 12:1—14:40.

Occasion for this section was misunderstanding and abuse of spiritual gifts. Those claiming most important gifts displayed them to humiliation of those with lesser gifts.

1. Heathen oracles compared with Christian revelation, 12:1-3. The oracles pretended revelation through idols, but "dumb" idols revealed nothing; only inspired men could say "Jesus is Lord."

2. Unity and purpose of spiritual gifts, 12:4-11.

a. Relation of the gifts to the Godhead, 4-6. To the Spirit—"gifts," "manifestation"; to Christ—"ministrations," or means of working; to God—"workings," or evidence of divine activity in the church.

This unity of gifts was against divisive use of them.

b. The gifts and their accomplishments, 7-11. They were nine in number, classified as follows:

(1) Those revealing the gospel: "Words of wisdom"—this gift used by apostles and prophets; "word of knowledge"—to teach revealed truths by inspired teachers; "prophecy"—to predict, see Acts 11:28; 21:8-11; "interpretation of tongues"—an essential in revealing truth; "discerning of spirits"—ability to distinguish false teachers from true, I John 4:1.

(2) Those confirming the gospel: "faith"—conviction they could work miracles, see Matt. 17:19-21; I Cor. 13:2; "healings"—power to restore the sick, Acts 5:15, 16; James 5:14, 15; "miracles"—examples in Acts 5:1-11; 13:8-11; "tongues"—ability to present the gospel in foreign languages, as on Pentecost, Acts 2:5-11.

Without these gifts not one of us would have the gospel, nor could we believe it.

3. Unity in using these gifts, 12:12-27.

a. Organic unity, 12, 13. As the human body "is one," so is the church; for by "one Spirit," directing through His word, we were all immersed into the one body.

b. Co-operative unity, 14-27. This, too, illustrated by the human body. Thus the sinful misuse of the gifts was exposed; they were given for the common good.

4. Gradation of gifts according to importance, 28-30. By ranking the spiritually gifted men in this order, precedence of each is settled.

A more excellent way than pride and strife about spiritual gifts is the manifestation of love.

5. Superiority of love in comparison with all spiritual gifts, 13:1-13.

a. The essential of love, 1-3: in speech—gift of tongues; in knowledge—to teach and predict; in faith—to work miracles; in giving—of goods and person.

b. The conduct of love, 4-7. It is personified in order to set forth its beauty and excellence in human relations.

c. The final values of love, 8-13. The following facts stand out:

(1) Prophecies, tongues, knowledge—and all the rest of the gifts—shall pass away when the "perfect" is come, namely, the gospel fully revealed and the church fully instructed, 8-10. The gifts came into the church through the apostles and went out with them.

(2) Progressive revelation to and instruction of the church during the apostolic age illustrated by development of childhood into manhood and by reflection of a mirror, 11, 12.

(3) Instead of spiritual gifts now we have faith, hope, love—the results from these gifts, 13. "Faith" is based on testimony of the Spirit, Rom. 10:17. "Hope" of the resurrection will be accomplished by the Spirit, Rom. 8:11. "Love" of God is imparted by the Spirit, Rom. 5:5, is the character of God, I John 4:16, hence eternal.

6. Superiority of prophecy to gift of tongues, 14:1-25.

This chapter corrects the selfish, vainglorious display of foreign tongues in the church at Corinth.

a. Comparison of prophesying and speaking in tongues, 1-5. Along with love spiritual gifts were desirable, but prophecy was superior to foreign tongues, because it edified (built up) the church in a known language.

b. The unprofitableness of speaking in a language not understood, 6-19. This is illustrated by sound without sense. Therefore inspired speaking, praying, singing in a foreign tongue must be interpreted, or the uninstructed could not say "Amen."

c. The significance of tongues and prophesying, 20-25. Misuse of gift of tongues was childish—a severe reproof to wiseacres in Corinth. Tongues had a twofold purpose: (a) ability to preach in foreign languages without learning them; (b) to prove the gospel of divine source. As Assyrian tongue was a sign to unbelieving Israel that their captivity was from God, so tongues in the church was a sign "to the unbelieving" "that God is among you," believers. However, tongues must be interpreted, or unbelievers will say "ye are mad." But intelligent prophetic preaching will convince.

7. Proper decorum in public worship, 14:26-40.

a. Number and order of speakers, 26-33. Edification of the church the one objective, hence there must be intelligent speech and division of time in use of the spiritual gifts, or confusion would result—a thing not attributive to God.

b. Women to keep silent in the assembly, 33-36. This for two reasons: 1. The law demands subjection, Gen. 3:16; Num. 30: 3-12. That is still in force, I Cor. 11:3. 2. Local custom, "shameful for a woman." Not so in the West. Even in early church were exceptions, Acts 21:9; I Cor. 11:5.

8. Final word on spiritual gifts, 37-40. His teaching is by authority of Christ, received by those willing to learn. Moreover, there is to be decent and orderly exercise of those gifts.

III. RESURRECTION OF THE DEAD, 15:1-58.

False teachers in Corinth denied the resurrection, vs. 12. Note Acts 17:32; 23:8. Foundational argument against this error is the resurrection of Christ.

1. The resurrection of Christ attested by Scriptures and eyewitnesses, 1-11. His resurrection gospel is delineated as:

"Preached," cp. Mark 16:15. No salvation without the gospel proclaimed.

"Received," because of its good news relative to sin and death, cp. Acts 2:41.

Limiting: "wherein ye stand," the boundary of Christian faith: all outside New Testament is illegal.

Saving—"saved, if": Men are saved and kept saved on conditions.

Factual, 3, 4. Hence no saving gospel before those events.

Witnessed, 5-11. Resurrection of Christ the fullest attested fact in history.

2. Denial of resurrection of the dead and consequences, 12-19. If no resurrection, what then?

"Christ hath not been raised." But see Matt. 28:6.

"Our preaching is vain"—void, empty of facts of the gospel (1-4). But see vs. 58.

"Your faith also is vain." It would be based on a dead Jew. But see John 14:19.

"We are found false witnesses." Their testimony was a living, seen Christ after His death; witnesses chosen of God, Acts 10:40-42. He cannot lie, Heb. 6:18.

"Ye are yet in your sins." Denial of Jesus' resurrection leaves a person without a Savior. But note Rom. 4:25; Heb. 7:25.

"The dead in Christ have perished." Without a raised Savior death ends all. But see John 11:25.

"We are of all men most pitiable." Christians endured suffering, loss of property and life. If hope ends in death they are most wretched and in need of pity. *"But now"*—

3. Resurrection of Christ guarantees all shall rise, 20-28. This is made certain: (a) By type, Lev. 23:9-14. As offering "first-fruits" of harvest sanctified the rest, so Christ "the first-fruits" from the dead set apart all men for resurrection. (b) By history. All die through Adam; all rise through Christ. Thus power of death is cancelled. (c) By order. Christ, the first-fruits, heads the list; next, His people; then "the end"—of death and Christ's reign.

4. Baptism in relation to the resurrection, 29. Baptism unites Christians with the risen Christ, Rom. 6:5. If no resurrection, this symbolism is nullified. Furthermore, in baptism we become members of the divine family, the living and the dead, Heb. 12:23. If no resurrection, this union with God's family is lost.

5. Hope of resurrection defies death, 30-34. If no resurrection, facing death on account of the gospel makes no sense.

6. Intellectual difficulties stated and met, 35-41. Rationalists

in Corinth argued impossibility of resurrection and raised two questions:

a. "How are the dead raised?" 35a. That is, how *can* they rise? Reply is by analogy as to *seed*, 36-38. (1) Seed produces by means of death, hence something is expected from the grave, 36. From death comes life. (2) Seed produces something greater and more excellent than itself, hence superiority of resurrected body to present body, 37. (3) Seed produces after its kind, hence from body will come body, 38. Conclusion is: Resurrection is possible. If God can produce vegetable life, He can produce immortality.

b. "With what manner of body do they come?" 35b. That is, with what *kind* of body do they come back? Will man lose his personal identity and cease to be human? Reply is by analogy as to *bodies*. (1) As there is diversity in bodies of flesh, yet common identity—all is *flesh,* so the resurrected body will be a material body constructed from the present body raised and modified for that purpose, hence human in form. (2) As there is diversity in glory of bodies celestial and terrestrial, yet a common identity (all is *glory*), so that resurrected body will be glorified, Phil. 3:20, 21.

From this it follows that man's personality, including spirit and body, will survive death. A body he must have to make him a complete man.

7. The earthly body and the resurrected body in contrast, 42-49. In characteristics the two are totally different, each adapted to its respective place of residence. These differences are caused by Adam first and Adam last.

8. Necessity of changing the earthly body into the resurrected body, 50-58. Reasons for change are: (a) "Flesh and blood cannot inherit the kingdom." Why? Rev. 21:1. Hence the dead are changed by resurrection, the living by transformation. (b) Victory over death. Then will be fulfilled, Isa. 25:8; Hos. 13:14. "The last enemy" shall be no more, Rev. 21:4. The exhortation is enforced by all facts in the chapter.

PART IV.
VARIOUS PRACTICAL DIRECTIONS, 16:1-24.

1. Concerning collection for the saints, 1-4. There was famine

in Judea, Acts 11:28-30. Collection for relief was called for among Macedonian churches. Four governing principles in giving, then and now: *time*—"the first day of the week"; *contributors*—"each one"; *place*—"lay by him in store" (treasury of church); *amount* —"as he may prosper."

2. Information about Paul's intended visit to Corinth, 5-9. He had purposed to visit Macedonia first, Corinth next, but after Pentecost, because of open door at Ephesus, see Acts 19:1-20.

3. Concerning Timothy and Apollos, 10-12. It seems young Timothy was fearful because of factionists in Corinth, hence request for kindness, for he would report the visit. Contrary to Paul's desire, Apollos postponed his visit, perhaps being displeased by factional use of his name.

4. Exhortation, 13, 14. Five imperatives summarize Paul's concern for the church because of difficulties named in the epistle.

5. Concerning Stephanas and companions, 15-18. They were delegates from Corinth with a letter to Paul, 7:1; cheered him with additional report, and in turn Paul refreshed the church; esteem highly such men.

6. Greetings, 19-24. These conveyed Christian love from churches of Asia, seven of which are named in Rev. 1:11; from Aquila and Prisca, then at Ephesus with Paul, Acts 18:18, 19; from Paul, attesting genuineness of the letter, with warning and benediction.

Second Letter to Corinth

INTRODUCTION.

1. Author. Paul's authorship is affirmed in 1:1. Its style is unmistakably Paul's, and the letter has undoubted connections with his life, with the church in Corinth and with the first letter.

2. Time and place of writing. It appears from 2:13; 7:5; 8:1; 9:2, 4, that Paul wrote this letter in A.D. 57, during his third missionary tour while in Macedonia.

3. Occasion and object of the letter. Having sent his first letter to Corinthians by their returning messengers, I Cor. 16:17, 18, Paul became exceedingly anxious as to its effect. It seems that he sent Titus with them as his own messenger, II Cor. 8:6. When Titus did not return, Paul, being greatly oppressed by forebodings of evil as to the church, crossed the sea from Troas into Macedonia, where he meets Titus. This second letter was called forth by the report brought by Titus, 7:5-14. It shows that the majority of the church was with Paul, but there was still a dangerous, defiant minority who accused Paul of changeableness, 1:15-20; self-laudation, 3:1; 5:12; 10:8; presumptuously claiming equality with the chief apostles, 12:11, 12; lack of eloquence, 11:6; an insignificant appearance, 10:10.

This letter was written to silence this bold and unscrupulous minority by answering their charges against him, also to exhort the church concerning the offering for the poor in Judea. In his first letter he weakened the opposition; in this he exterminates it.

The inner life of Paul is more fully revealed here than elsewhere, and that gives the principal value of this letter to us. It portrays him as a worker in suffering, love and consciousness of divine authority conferred upon him.

ANALYSIS AND NOTES

INTRODUCTION, 1:1-11.

1. Salutation, 1, 2. Affirmation of apostolic authority needed because denied in Corinth; Timothy, well known, was joint-sender of this circular letter; good will of "grace" and "peace" would be effective.

2. Thanksgiving for comfort and deliverance, 3-11.

a. The God of all comfort in affliction, 3-7. A threefold revelation of God is given. He is: Father of Jesus—not Joseph, cp. Matt. 1:18; Father of mercies—suffers with His children, Isa. 63:9; God of all comfort—through words of His Spirit, John 14:16, 17; Acts 9:31. This comfort in trouble is to be passed on.

b. Paul's afflictions in Asia and deliverance, 8-11. Account given in Acts 19:23-41. In the face of certain death two instruments secured his deliverance: "God," and "ye also" by prayer.

PART I.
PAUL'S DEFENSE AND APOSTOLIC MISSION
1:12—7:16.

His traducers in Corinth necessitated this action.

I. HIS CONDUCT AND HOW GOVERNED, 1:12-14. Paul's defense is testimony of "conscience" directed by word of God, not by worldly wisdom and policy, cp. Acts 23:1. What he wrote has no other meaning "than what ye read"—no hidden sinister purpose.

II. HIS INTENDED VISIT TO CORINTH MODIFIED AND DEFENDED, 1:15—2:13.

1. Change of plan. (a) Original plan, 15, 16. To visit Corinth first, Macedonia next; to visit them twice; to visit them soon. (b) Changed plan, I Cor. 16:5-8. To visit Macedonia first; to visit Corinth once; to wait until after Pentecost. This alteration led Paul's enemies to accuse him of "fickleness," hence unreliable.

2. The change defended, 1:17—2:13.

a. He is not guilty of promise-breaking, 17-22. Two reasons:

he is like the unchangeable Christ he proclaims; he has the stamp of God's approval by the Holy Spirit.

b. He delayed his visit in order to give Corinthians time to repent and thus escape discipline, 1:23—2:4. Many were their sins as recorded in first letter, penned "with many tears."

c. The incestuous man, one reason for delay, having repented, is to be forgiven by the church, 2:5-11. This is done by receiving him back into fellowship.

d. He goes into Macedonia to meet Titus and get report from Corinth, 2:12, 13. It brought great joy, 7:5-7.

III. HIS BLAMELESS LIFE, SEEN IN THE GOSPEL MINISTRY, 2:14—7:16.

1. Triumphant through Christ, 2:14-17. This by the gospel, a savor (fragrance) to saved and perishing; moreover by an uncorrupted gospel, hence unlike the false teachers.

2. The commendatory fact of the church in Corinth, 3:1-5. Evidently false teachers submitted letters of commendation. The church founded by Paul was his letter, composed by Christ, penned "by us," inked by the Holy Spirit who inspired us, inscribed on "hearts of flesh" through faith and obedience, addressed to "all men."

3. His ministry of a better covenant, 3:6-18. Inferiority of old covenant to new appears:

In *ministration*—old by Moses, new by apostles, 6.

In *character*—old is letter, new is Spirit, 6.

In *effect*—old brought death, new gives life, 6.

In *glory*—old came with glory, Ex. 34:29; new more glorious, 7-11.

In *purpose*—old veiled Christ in types and figures, symbolized by Moses' veil; new reveals Christ, "the end" or object of the law, 13, cp. Gal. 3:24.

In *duration*—old done away in Christ, 11, 14, see Rom. 10:4; new remains.

Explanatory. This concerns: (a) The Jews. Through unbelief their present condition is hardened mind and veiled spiritual eyes, 14, 15. But as Moses appeared before God with veil removed, Ex. 34:34, so when Israel turns to Christ their veil will drop. (b) The new covenant. "The Lord is the Spirit," 17; but the Spirit is the new covenant, 6; therefore Christ is the new covenant. See Isa. 42:6, 7. (c) The apostles, 18. Unlike Moses, "we" apostles have no veil but reflect, like a mirror, the glory of the Lord which causes increasing transformation of men.

4. A commendable ministry, 4:1-6. "This ministry," of reflecting the glory of the Lord, 3:18, is courageous, open and above board, honest, manifesting the truth—unveiled except to unbelievers. Not self, but Christ is proclaimed who inspired in us the message.

5. A ministry of suffering and divine support, 4:7-15. Effect of the gospel is not in preachers, for they are like earthen vessels subject to breaking, 7; warriors defending a treasure, 8, 9; typically re-enacting the death and resurrection of Christ, 10-15.

6. Reasons for courageously facing the ills of life, 4:16—5:10. We never lose heart because: (a) present afflictions are outweighed by eternal glory, 16-18; (b) expecting the resurrection body and home with the Lord, 5:1-10. The present body (in the Greek a tent-house, hence "the house of my pilgrimage," Ps. 119:54) will be replaced by a permanent building—the resurrection body, guaranteed by the gift of the Spirit. Therefore death has no terror; our one aim is to please God, in view of coming judgment.

7. The Apostle's motives for living, 11-21. They are: (a) "The fear of the Lord," 11-13. In view of the judgment, his work was persuasion of men, not "again" (3:1) self-commendation—the answer to his proud critics. (b) The love of Christ, 14, 15. He died for all, hence all should live for Him. (c) No distinction among men, 16-19. "All have sinned," Rom. 3:22; Christ died for all; He gives a new view of life and things, all according to God's plan and for reconciliation. (d) Apostles are ambassadors, 20, 21. An official position conferred on apostles only as Christ's representatives who speak for Him. See Matt. 16:18; John 20:22, 23. Hence they alone can offer reconciliation to God through atonement of Christ.

8. Appeal, 6:1—7:16.

a. "The grace of God," 6:1-13. As Christ's ambassador and co-worker Paul entreats not to defeat the grace of God by a life of sin, cp. Titus 2:11, 12. Grace came when most needed and rendered help, 1, 2.

The appeal is enforced by personal suffering, 3-5; by special virtues, 6-13. This was a moving exhortation, far beyond experience of his critics.

b. "Come ye out," 6:14—7:1. A call for complete break with paganism in marriage and unclean practices, thus "perfecting holiness in the fear of God."

c. "Open your hearts," 7:2-16. Receive me as a true apostle of Christ because of: (1) Deserving conduct and inseparable love, 2-4. Together we live and die. (2) Improved condition of the church resulting from former letter, 5-16. It induced repentance, especially manifested in discipline of the incestuous man. This test case vindicated Paul as an apostle of Christ, 12, and proved his hopeful words to Titus concerning the Corinthians, 14, 15.

PART II.
EXHORTATION CONCERNING OFFERING FOR BRETHREN IN JUDEA,
8:1—9:15.

In I Cor. 16:1-3 Paul gave plan of procedure; now he urges the church to "complete the doing."

I. MOTIVES FOR GIVING, 8:1—9:5.

1. The example of Macedonians, 1-7. The following is observed: power of example, cp. Mark 12:41-44; "liberality," despite poverty from persecution; "first"—the beginning and cause; "grace"—in 1, 9, disposition—in 4, 6, 7, 19, the offering.

2. Giving a test of love, 8-12. Unlike the law, the gospel does not command giving; it is motivated by Christ—His love for us and ours for Him. See Phil. 2:6-8; Matt. 8:20.

3. The principle of equality, 13-15. It is a two-way principle, illustrated by the manna, Ex. 16:17, 18.

4. The offering committee, 16-24. This consisted of Titus, a "brother," and seven others, Acts 20:2-6. They gathered the offering, took it to Jerusalem and thus cleared Paul of any suspicion in the matter.

5. The example of Corinthians, 9:1-5. Their zeal "stirred up" Macedonia; Titus and "brother," 8:16, 18, are sent in ad-

vance to ready Corinth, lest there be humiliation if some from Macedonia should come with Paul.

II. ENCOURAGEMENTS TO GIVE AND RESULTS, 9:6-15.

1. Bountifully, 6. Enforced by law of sowing and reaping.

2. Cheerfully, 7. The word derived from Greek *hilaron,* from which hilarious, joyous. No grudged gift should be received.

3. Giving multiplies means for giving, 8-11. The assurance is "God is able"—as in nature, so in charity. With Ps. 112:9, cp. Prov. 19:17.

4. The effect, 12-15. The offering met needs of the saints, with thanksgiving; God was glorified by obedience of the gospel confession; racial prejudice was broken down—all one in Christ. The cause of it all the "unspeakable gift," 8:5.

OBSERVATION.

Paul's letters to Corinthians contain the most comprehensive treatise on giving found in the New Testament. Although intended for relief of the poor, its principles are applicable to all church giving, benevolence being just one item.

PART III.
DEFENSE OF HIS APOSTLESHIP AND ANNOUNCEMENT OF HIS COMING
10:1—13:14.

The previous portion of the letter was addressed primarily to the church as a whole; this part is addressed especially to his enemies.

I. HIS POWER AND AUTHORITY COMPARED WITH OPPOSERS, 10:1-18.

1. Ultimatum to the opposition, 1-6. With meekness and gentleness of Christ Paul meets ridicule of opponents who said he was meek when present but bold by letter. However, he is not a coward when courage is needed. And his weapons are not

of human kind, but divine power "to avenge all disobedience" —a victory effective locally and world-wide.

2. Vindication through comparison, 7-18.

a. As to being Christ's apostle, 7. Unlike the false teachers, Paul was a qualified apostle by having seen Christ, Acts 9:3-6.

b. As to apostolic authority and power, 8-12. It was given for edification of Corinthians, not destruction; but, if brought to test, he would not be shamed before his slanderers who compared and measured themselves with each other instead of Christ.

c. As to divinely appointed territory, 13-18. Christ sent Paul to Gentiles, Acts 26:16-18, and that included Corinth and beyond. He did not enter territory prepared by others, as did his opposers; hence, unlike them, he could boast as one commended by the Lord.

II. HIS SELF-COMMENDATION, 11:1—12:13.

1. Apology for boasting, 1-4. Having the Lord's approval, 10:18, self-praise would appear foolish, but affection for them compelled. He had betrothed them to Christ; he feared that, as Eve was beguiled, so Corinthians would be deceived by false teachers, for they could offer no other Jesus, Spirit or gospel than Paul had preached.

2. Defensive boasting, 11:5—12:10.

a. Comparison with false apostles, 5, 6; note 13. In rank he measures up; although untrained in speech, cp. I Cor. 2:4, not so in knowledge.

b. Preaching without pay, 7-15. Enemies denied his apostleship on ground he did not ask wages. Paul meets charge by: (1) he did not want to burden, but save Corinthians; so "other churches," see Phil. 4:15, 16, and "the brethren" Silas and Timothy, Acts 18:5, provided his support—a disgrace to the church, hence vs. 11; (2) he would not be example to those who wanted pay, for they were not apostles of Christ but of Satan.

3. Further apology for boasting, 11:16—12:10.

a. Labor and suffering, 16-33. This distasteful self-advertising was not of the Lord but was necessitated by enemies who gloried "after the flesh" and was tolerated by the church, hence Paul asks for toleration. Then follows an extensive, direct challenge his enemies could not meet.

b. Visions and revelations, 12:1-10. In Bible times some truth was revealed by visions. In relation to Paul there was: (1) Experience, 1-6. Since this letter was written in 57, fourteen years back would place Paul in Antioch of Syria, Acts 11:25, 26; revelation came independent of his body; for example of supernatural experience *in* the body see Acts 8:39, 40, *out* of the body, Ezek. 8:3; place of revelation, "third" heaven. According to Jewish speaking, "first" heaven is the air, "second" where planets are, "third" where God is. (2) Restraint, 7-10. Purpose was to keep him humble; character of the thorn is unknown, but Satan, as in case of Job (2:6, 7), was permitted to afflict; suffering was compensated by power of Christ.

4. Reason for boasting, 11-13. "Ye compelled me" by failure to defend me in face of supernatural proof of my apostleship. Compared with other churches, your only inferiority is I preached to you without charge. "Forgive me this wrong."

III. HIS THIRD VISIT TO CORINTH AND FINAL WORD, 12:14—13:14.

1. Motive of his visit, 14-18. "Not yours, but you." Reimbursement for past labors he declined because of parental duty to children—he was their spiritual father, I Cor. 4:14, 15, and only asks love. Nevertheless, enemies accused him of "guile"—misappropriation to self the offering for Judea; Titus and the brother are his defense.

2. Misconception of his letter corrected, 19-21. They misconstrued Paul's lengthy defense to be his excuse, whereas he penned it in the sight of God for their much-needed edification and reformation. Partisan feeling, and impurity, still plagued the church.

3. Warning of rigorous discipline, 13:1-10. By legal procedure his second-visit warning will be enforced without leniency —a proof of Christ speaking in him. Therefore they are to test their faith and conduct as to whether they are Christians, then they would find he also is a Christian, for he could do nothing against the truth. According to their opinion he may be weak and they strong; however, his prayer is for their perfection, hence

purpose of letter and warning is to build up, not to cast down.

4. Conclusion, 11-14. With brotherly affection the church is urged to go on to perfection, to enjoy comfort of the gospel, to think alike by means of the word, to live in peace among themselves, and thus to enjoy the presence of God.

The most comprehensive benediction in the New Testament is remarkable in view of what the apostle was compelled to write to this disorderly church. It is of interest to compare the apostolic benediction with the priestly of the Jewish religion, recorded in Numbers 6:24-26. The parallels are there.

Letter to the Galatians

INTRODUCTION.

1. The land and people. Galatia was a rough, mountainous region in central Asia Minor. The inhabitants were a mixed people of Gauls, Greeks and Jews. The Gauls seem to have been in majority. Their characteristics are described by Julius Caesar, who says: "The infirmity of the Gauls is that they are fickle in their resolves, and fond of change, and not to be trusted." This agrees with Gal. 1:6; 3:1.

2. The letter.

a. Authorship and date. Paul was the author, 1:1; 6:11. The date was about A.D. 57, during his third evangelistic tour, most probably from Corinth, certainly after the conference in Jerusalem, A.D. 50, Acts 15; Gal. 2:1-10.

b. Persons addressed. Of Paul's epistles this is the only one written to a group of churches, including Antioch, Iconium, Lystra and Derbe, hence a circular letter.

c. The purpose.

(1) To overcome the influence of Judaizing teachers in order that the Galatian Christians may continue in Christ. To this end Paul proves his gospel of divine source and shows difference between the law and the gospel.

(2) To establish his apostleship. In order to succeed, the Judaizers felt necessity of denying Paul was an apostle of Christ. This Paul meets by declaring his divine appointment to the apostleship.

3. Relation of Galatians to Romans. In both Paul discusses relation of the law to the gospel and proves that we are justified, not by works of the law, but by obedience of faith. This necessitated comparison of Christianity with Judaism.

Galatians is the key to New Testament apologetics. Around it are grouped Romans and I and II Corinthians. These deal with the critical questions of the apostolic age and ours.

This epistle was Luther's trumpet by which he sounded *liberty* to Christians from the papal hierarchy, 5:1. By Romans he proclaimed *life* by faith, 1:17, instead of works of penance.

ANALYSIS AND NOTES

INTRODUCTION, 1:1-10.

1. Personal greetings, 1-5. Paul meets challenge of his apostleship by affirming its divine source and agency, backed by co-workers, 1, 2.

Salutation in 3-5 contains motives for steadfastness in Christ. "He gave himself for our sins" in order to *rescue,* same verb in Acts 23:27. The world is wrecked and sinking. Rescue was God-planned, hence perfect and successful. Christians are in the wisdom and will of God!

2. Occasion of the letter, 6-10. There was removal to a different gospel which was no gospel at all, proclaimed by perverters who mixed law and gospel—penalized by "anathema"—cut off from God and His church; this pronouncement was at expense of human friendship but done by a servant of Christ.

PART I.
PAUL'S DEFENSE OF HIS APOSTLESHIP AND GOSPEL, 1:11—2:21.

1. His gospel and apostleship divinely derived, 1:11-24.

a. The divine origin of his gospel, 11, 12. It came, not as a human product, nor by human teaching, but through revelation of Jesus Christ.

b. Proof of its divine origin, 13-24. (1) His early life contrary to the gospel, 13, 14. Hence *he* could not have originated it. Cp. Acts 8:3; 9:1. (2) His separation, call and early preaching not from men, 15-17. Hence he must be an apostle of Christ and taught by Him. Note Acts 9:20. (3) His visit to Jerusalem not long enough for instruction in the gospel, 18-24. Hence did not learn it in school—fifteen days insufficient for course in Bible college, yet had knowledge to preach abroad.

2. His gospel and apostleship confirmed and maintained, 2:1-21.

a. Confirmed by the hand of fellowship at Jerusalem, 1-10. "Fourteen years" from his call he went as delegate from Antioch, Syria, to conference at Jerusalem, Acts 15:1-35. "False brethren" were teaching Gentiles must be circumcised in order to be saved. Paul opposed, backed by the conference and right hand of fellowship by apostles, thereby acknowledging his gospel and apostleship.

b. Maintained in conflict with Peter at Antioch, 11-21. The situation reveals: (1) Hypocritical conduct of Peter and others, 11-13. Despite Peter's vision, Acts 10:9-16, and decision of conference at Jerusalem, he from fear withdrew from Gentile Christians when Judaizers came from Jerusalem; even Barnabas, note Acts 11:24, with others "dissembled" (Greek, acted hypocrites). (2) Paul's reproof, 14-21. Peter's sinful action in turning back to the law made Christ out to be a "minister," promoter, of sin. See Rom. 3:20. "God forbid." So then return to the law is transgression; besides, Christians are dead to the law, having been crucified with Christ, cp. Rom. 7:4, and now live by faith in Him. Thus Paul vindicates his apostolic authority.

N.B. Here the first pope, if he was one, is rebuked by an apostle, thus annihilating claim of infallibility.

Inspiration of the apostles had to do, not with *conduct*, but with *inspiration* of message, John 16:13.

PART II.
JUSTIFICATION, NOT BY THE LAW, BUT BY FAITH IN CHRIST, 3:1—4:31.

The proposition is proved:

1. By reception of the Holy Spirit, 3:1-5. Galatians' irrational return to Judaism was exposed by their own experience. Their folly is pointed out by reception of the Spirit; by going backward instead of forward; by having suffered in vain as Christians; by knowing that God bestowed the Spirit and worked miracles, not by the law, but by the gospel.

2. By the case of Abraham, 6-9. As Abraham was declared righteous through faith in God concerning descendants, Gen. 15:5, 6, so Gentiles and Jews are blessed through faith in and obedience to Christ.

3. By inability of the law to justify, 10-12. It brought mankind under "curse" of death and left them there, Deut. 27:26; only by gospel faith can they come alive.

4. By the death of Christ, 13, 14. He redeemed from curse of law by becoming its penalty, II Cor. 5:15, 21, thus secured for Jews and Gentiles the blessing of Abraham, Gen. 12:3.

5. By superiority of the gospel to the law, 15-29.

a. Illustrated and proved by covenant with Abraham, 15-18. As man's covenant, once ratified, remains in force, so God's covenant with Abraham concerning his "seed, which is Christ," confirmed by His oath, Gen. 22:16, was not nullified by the law 430 years later; hence "inheritance" of the world, Rom. 4:13, is not by the law but by faith of the gospel.

b. Seen in the law as a temporary arrangement, 19-29. As such it was "added" to covenant with Abraham as a restraining factor, I Tim. 1:9, "till the seed should come"; is not against gospel "promises" because it could not give life, hence people under it were "shut up" for 1,500 years like prisoners doomed to death until released by Christ through faith in and immersion "into" Him. Thus He is for all Christians the unit of unity.

6. By illustrations why the law preceded and must give way to the gospel, 4:1-31.

a. Childhood and manhood, 1-11. There is here resumption of metaphor in 3:24. There the law is "tutor," child-trainer; here person under the law is like a child under "guardians" as to person and "stewards" as to property "until the day appointed by the father" in his will, which corresponds to "the fulness of the time" when Christ came to "redeem" from under the law, bring adoption into the divine family and thus become heirs, Rom. 8:17.

"However" the Gentiles, 8-11, having left paganism with its gods and ceremonies, were persuaded by Judaizers to observe with them the special seasons of the law—a condition which gave anxiety to Paul.

b. Appeal, 12-20. It is based on: his personal example of faith and friendship, 12; their former affection for him, 13-16; the proselyting Jews, 17, 18, showing pretended affection with wrong purpose, cp. Matt. 23:15; Paul's tender affection and painful anxiety, 19, 20.

    c.   Sarah and Hagar, 21-31. This allegory was intended to exterminate the Judaizing teachers with their own weapon and to correct errors of followers. Points of comparison appear thus:

  (1) Mothers.
      (a) The handmaid—old covenant, 24.
      (b) The freewoman—new covenant, 26, 31.
  (2) Sons.
      (a) As representatives.
          1. Ishmael—Jews of the old.
          2. Isaac—Christians of the new.
      (b) Births.
          1. Ishmael—natural under the old, 29.
          2. Isaac—spiritual under the new, 29, note 28.
      (c) Dispositions.
          1. Ishmael—Jewish persecution, 29.
          2. Isaac—Christian endurance, 29.
      (d) Status.
          1. Ishmael—bondage of the old, 25.
          2. Isaac—freedom of the new, 31.
      (e) Inheritance.
          1. Ishmael—rejection of Jews, 30. Note Romans chapters 9, 10.
          2. Isaac—acceptance of Christians, 30.

PART III.
EXHORTATION TO STEADFASTNESS, HOLINESS AND DUTY, 5:1—6:18.

Having proved in chapters 3, 4, that Christians are not under the law, the application is now enforced by exhortation.

1. Freedom of the gospel, 5:1-12. Freedom and responsibility, 1, therefore "stand fast."

Circumcision and alternatives, 2-6. If circumcised: "Christ will profit you nothing," you are "debtor to the whole law," you are "severed from Christ," you have "fallen away from grace."

Interrupted progress, 7-10. Illustrated by "running" and "leaven," yet confidence expressed.

Self-defense, 11, 12. Persecution of Paul proved he did not preach circumcision as charged.

2. Limitation of freedom, 5:13-15. It is not for gratification of fleshly lusts, but for service through love, instead of hateful, beastlike party spirit.

3. Victory over the flesh, 16-26. The Christian is between two mighty forces—*"flesh"* and *"Spirit"—lusting* (longing) for possession. Here is a fierce tug of war. Who wins? The Spirit's victory is certain through His *word* by which the Christian is said to "walk," be "led," and "live"; thus the flesh is "crucified" —put to death.

4. Duties of the church, 6:1-10.

a. To those who yield to the flesh, 1-5. The erring Christian is to be restored gently, 1; sympathetically, 2; humbly, 3-5.

b. To the gospel teacher, 6-10. The instructed is to "communicate"—(share) money and goods, 6; obligation enforced by inflexible law of sowing and reaping as to: (1) *what* we sow, 7; (b) *where* we sow, 7; (3) *when* we reap, 9. Moreover, sharing means doing good to "all men," especially those in the church, 10.

CONCLUSION, 6:11-18.

1. Token of authorship, 11. The amanuensis turns over the the pen to Paul, cp. II Thess. 3:17.

2. Motives of Judaizers and Paul, 12-16. Theirs, zeal for self-glory, not for keeping the law; Paul's, the cross of Christ, productive of a new creature. Hence "this rule" (yardstick) is measurement of life. On this account Paul, like a Roman slave, was branded by persecution as the property of Christ.

3. Benediction, 18. Despite knockout blows against Judaizers, Paul addressed them as "brethren," invoking the favor of the Lord.

Letter to the Ephesians

INTRODUCTION.

1. Author and date. The letter is claimed by Paul, the prisoner, 3:1; 4:1; 6:20. According to chronology in Acts of Apostles his first imprisonment in Rome lasted from A.D. 61 to 63, In that time he wrote four letters: Ephesians, Philippians, Colossians, Philemon. The approximate date for Ephesians would be A.D. 62.

2. The church at Ephesus. Paul's first visit was short, Acts 18:19, 20, but Priscilla and Aquila were left there to carry on the work begun. On his second visit he remained there two years and three months, Acts 19:8, 10. Altogether he spent three years there, Acts 20:31, a longer time than in any other place. It was a long and hard battle (Acts 19), but all the forces of iniquity were no match against the preaching of one man. "All they that dwelt in Asia heard the word of the Lord," and a strong church was the result.

3. The design of the epistle. It is primarily a treatise on the church. According to God's eternal purpose, Christ is its originator, head and foundation. It is inclusive of Jews and Gentiles, hence unifies all peoples in Christ. Its character and conduct demand a complete break with the old life of sin which entails a constant warfare against spiritual hosts of wickedness whose defeat is assured.

ANALYSIS AND NOTES

INTRODUCTION, 1:1, 2.

1. Inscription, 1. Paul signs himself as an apostle of Christ according to God's will, not human appointment, see Acts 26:15,

16. Persons addressed are saints at Ephesus and believers in Christ everywhere.

2. Salutation, 2. Favor and peace from God and Christ are the good wishes for the church.

PART I.
BLESSINGS OF GOD THROUGH CHRIST IN THE CHURCH, 1:3—3:21.

1. Redemption through Christ, 1:3-14.

a. Enjoyed in the church, 3. There praise to God is offered for "every spiritual blessing," nothing is lacking. The church is styled "the heavenly places in Christ" because it is "the kingdom of heaven" (Matt. 16:18, 19) where is "our citizenship" (Phil. 3:20), but with responsibility on earth.

b. Predetermined 4-6. Before the creation of the world (cp. II Tim. 1:9) God had purposed to bless all peoples, Jews and Gentiles, in Christ through process of adoption. This should call forth praise for His amazing goodness.

c. Secured through Christ's death, 7. Without His shed blood there can be no deliverance from sin, Rev. 1:5.

d. Made known, 8, 9. The secret of redemption was made known to the apostles, hence is no longer a mystery of the old covenant. They have told the world.

e. Experienced, 10-14. All things of the gospel dispensation are summed up in Christ. Those who receive Him are "made a heritage," Rom. 8:17; "having heard the word of the truth," they believe in Christ; their heavenly inheritance is attested and guaranteed by the Holy Spirit, Acts 2:38b, and so is also their redemption from the grave, Rom. 8:23: all of which redounds to the eternal praise of Christ, Rev. 5:12.

2. Prayer for the saints in Christ, 1:15-23.

a. The reason, 15, 16. Faith in Christ retained; love of the saints continued.

b. The petition, 17-23. For the Spirit of wisdom and revelation unto full knowledge of God, cp. Col. 1:9. That ye may know:

The *hope* of his calling, i.e., the hope of the gospel, Col. 1:23.

The *riches* of inheritance, I Cor. 2:9; I Pet. 1:4.

The *power* for believers, the immeasurable power of the Holy

Spirit which raised Christ from the dead to be the ruler of the universe, the church included.

3. Their past and present condition, 2:1-22.

a. Dead, but made alive, 1-10.

Were dead through sin, 1-3. By yielding to Satan in lusts of the flesh. Cp. Jas. 1:15.

Were made alive through Christ, 4-10. This God did because of mercy, love and grace which resulted in a spiritual resurrection, John 5:25; Rom. 6:4; Titus 3:5.

Thus salvation is God's "gift," neuter gender, not "faith," which is feminine.

b. Separated, but brought near, 11-22.

To God, 11-13. Though separated, alienated, strangers, godless, yet now near by the blood of Christ, the only way to God, Heb. 10:19, 20.

To one another, 14-18. Death of Christ not only joined people to God but also Jews and Gentiles to each other by removing the law between them, thus unifying them in peace. Jesus only is God's plan for "One World" and one household of faith. He alone can make the "new man."

Hence Christians are no longer strangers and sojourners. The church is a community of home-dwellers, having a common interest. They live in "the city of the living God" (Heb. 12:22), founded upon apostles, Christian prophets (note 3:5), and Christ himself. This speaks security, and also authority in the church, the habitation of God through the Spirit, John 14:23.

4. The mystery of Christ relative to the Gentiles, 3:1-21.

a. It caused Paul's imprisonment, 1, 2. Creating Jews and Gentiles into "one new man" (2:15) was offensive to Jews and caused Paul's imprisonment at Caesarea and Rome (see Acts of Apostles).

b. It was made known, 3-13:

By revelation, 3a. The only way men can know God's purpose and plan.

By writing, 3b-6. Thus God's revelation is passed on to the future—"when ye *read.*" The mystery of Christ relative to the Gentiles, not fully known before Christ, but now made known by His apostles and prophets.

By preaching, 7-9. This will "make all men *see*" *(Greek,* to turn on the light). The gospel is God's light, II Cor. 4:4.

By the church, 10-12. Even the angels did not know God's eternal purpose, though they had looked into it before the church, I Pet. 1:12.

With confidence in God's purpose Paul asked the Ephesians not to lose heart, for what he suffered was for their glory, 13.

c. Paul's prayer in their behalf, 14-19. This remarkable petition is concerned with:

Strength of the Spirit, 16. He is not only in His word but also in the church, I Cor. 3:16. By this power she goes forward or not at all.

The indwelling Christ, 17a. That cuts out self, Gal. 2:20. Christ's presence through the Holy Spirit, His representative on earth, gives confidence: "Lo, I am with you." It is a matter of "faith," and "faith is assurance," Heb. 11:1.

The dimensions of the church, 17b, 18. It is the sum of the eternal purpose in Christ, it being His spiritual body. Because its members are rooted in the soil of love, the prayer is that they may fully comprehend the church, the product of divine love, 5:25. Under figure of a building, how great is the church? In length and breadth its plan covers the whole earth; in depth it reaches the foundation Christ; in height it reaches up to heaven, being the entrance into "the Holy of holies." (See Jewish Tabernacle).

The love of Christ, 19a. It is boundless, yet can be known by the church according to limitations of its members; is conveyed by the word and the Spirit, John 3:16; Rom. 5:5.

The fulness of God, 19b. In a special sense the spiritual gifts in the early church were His fulness, I Cor. 12:4-11. Though not in the church now, yet the church is "the habitation of God in (by) the Spirit," 2:22.

The benediction, 20, 21. Much as God has done, He can still do more; there is no limit to His power in the church. For all His blessings He is to be glorified through the eternal ages.

PART II.
UNITY OF THE CHURCH, 4:1-16.

1. Appeal, 1-3. Coming from a prisoner for preaching Christ, it has unusual persuasive power—

a. To walk worthily, 1, 2. Because they are members of Christ, I Cor. 6:15, and children of God, I John 2:1, they are highly honored. The worthy walk also includes consideration of each other. Christ is the pattern, II Cor. 10:1.

b. To keep the unity of the Spirit, 3. Diligence means to hasten, to exert one's self in regard to unity. The matter is urgent, John 17:20, 21. The power of unity is the Holy Spirit, retained by the bond of peace among Christians.

2. Basic unity, 4-6. There are seven unities:

a. One body, not several. The body is the church, 1:22, 23. Christians are unified in Christ by faith in and obedience to Him, Gal. 3:27. Thus they become *one* church, not several denominations as now. In relation to each other they are "brethren," Matt. 23:8, and should dwell together in unity, Ps. 133:1.

b. One Spirit, not several. It is the Holy Spirit who is in the body to give it life and power and to create a holy character in its members, Gal. 5:22, 23. Denominationalism cannot keep the unity of the Spirit. Each division has its own peculiar Spirit.

c. One hope. It is the hope of the resurrection and future life, Acts 26:6-8; Col. 1:27. Those who deny Christ and the resurrection are of all men most pitiable.

d. One Lord, not several. Christ alone is Lord and Head of the church, Acts 2:36. He rules out all human authority in the church. Before Him only men stand or fall.

e. One faith, not several. It is the faith of the gospel, styled "the word of faith," Rom. 10:8, because it produces faith, 17, and is all sufficient, II Tim. 3:16, 17. The church is obligated to keep the unity of that faith without creedal addition or subtraction.

f. One baptism, not several. It is immersion in water of a penitent believer in the name of Jesus Christ unto remission of past sins, Acts 2:38. The authority of Christ shuts out the several "modes" of baptism now in vogue.

g. One God, not several like gods and lords of paganism, I

Cor. 8:5, 6. Nor must modern Pope and Saint worship detract from the one God.

3. Growing unity, 4:7-16. Christ gave certain persons to the church for instruction with reference to service, converts, unity, knowledge, maturity in Christ "that we may be no longer children."

PART III.
CHRISTIAN CONDUCT IN THE CHURCH, 4:17—6:9.

1. Individual conduct, 4:17—5:21.

a. Not as the Gentiles, 4:17-24. They walk in vanity, i.e., emptiness, nothingness, mentally and morally, because they are in the dark. Christians are different, having been enlightened by truth in Christ. Put off, therefore, as unclean garments, the old man of sin, and put on the new-created man.

b. But as a renewed people, 4:25—5:21.

In relation to each other, 4:25-32. One member cannot work against another. "Love worketh no ill to his neighbor," Rom. 13:10.

In character as saints, 5:1-14. Without it no inheritance in the eternal kingdom, hence "walk as children of light." Cp. Rom. 12:2.

In economy of time, 15-21. "Redeeming" (a word from the market-place) idea is to buy up time and opportunities for holy living, because of evil days. Time is the essence of our covenant with Christ, therefore we must get busy. Not riotous living, but a life in the Spirit.

2. Family conduct, 5:22—6:9.

a. Husband and wife, 5:22-33. In wedlock is mutual obligation.

The wife submits to the husband, 22-24. This is done "as to the Lord," not merely as to the husband. Yet the wife is in subjection to the husband as is the church to Christ.

The husband loves the wife, 25-33. The pattern set is Christ's love for the church—even unto death. The aim was cleansing it through the bath of regeneration by means of the word. Cp.

Titus 3:5. The final aim is a glorious, spotless church. Furthermore, the husband loves his wife because of unity in wedlock: "no man ever hated his own flesh," cp. Gen. 2:23, 24.

Altogether, marriage is analogous of the eternal union of the church with Christ in submission and adorable love.

b. Parents and children, 6:1-4. Children's obedience is bounded by Christ and His word. Two motives: It is *"right"* —God has commanded it, Prov. 23:32; it has *"promise"*—well-being and long life.

Parents' obligations are: *"provoke not"* by unreasonable demands and harsh language, cp. Col. 3:2; *"nurture them"*—bring them up by discipline and instruction of the Lord.

c. Servants, 6:5-9. Rome had its slaves, the gospel respects civil government, Rom. 13:1, 2. Christian slaves must render service "as unto Christ"; they are His slaves, cp. Gal. 1:10. Christian masters are to reciprocate in treatment of slaves; both have the same master in heaven. Incidentally, these principles are applicable to modern capital and labor.

PART IV.
THE MILITANT CHURCH, 6:10-20.

Victory is assured through:

1. Strength in the Lord, 10-17. This is found in complete armor of God, not for the body but for the mind, cp. II Cor. 10:4. The stake is eternal life, I Tim. 6:12. A hostile, spiritual universe surrounds the Christian, and in order to withstand the diabolical powers the *whole* armor is necessary, not merely single pieces. Each serves a definite purpose.

2. Prayer in the Spirit, 18-20. This is the Christian soldier on guard—"watching"; It is to be practiced at all seasons; it is motivated and taught by the Holy Spirit; and it is in behalf of all men, the preacher included.

CONCLUSION, 6:21-24.

1. Tychicus the messenger, 21, 22. A former associate of Paul, Acts 20:4, now in Rome. As bearer of the epistle he would bring information concerning Paul—his preaching and treatment. See Acts 28:23-30.

2. Benediction, 23, 24. A twofold wish is expressed: First, "peace" to the brethren, resulting in love and faith, 23. Second, "grace" to all sincere lovers of Christ. Otherwise it is "anathema," I Cor. 16:22.

Letter to the Philippians

INTRODUCTION.

1. The author and date. Paul the author was in "bonds" (1:19) in Rome, indicated by greetings "from Caesar's household" (4:22). He wrote it during his first imprisonment about A.D. 62.

2. The church at Philippi. The graphic account of its origin is found in Acts 16:11-40. Paul's companions were Silas, Luke and Timothy; the Holy Spirit selected the territory for evangelism; the plea of a man in a vision gave direction; the beginning of preaching was at the riverside; expulsion of a spirit of divination caused persecution and imprisonment of Paul and Silas; then conversion of the jailer and release of the prisoners—all of which makes introduction of the gospel into Europe a most exciting drama.

3. The occasion of the letter. It was written in grateful acknowledgment of help from the church when the apostle suffered want while a prisoner (4:18). Besides its practical teaching and admonition, it discloses a heartfelt, touching affection for his brethren. That makes it essentially a personal letter to his children in the gospel, hence its contents may be conveniently seen in the common chapter divisions.

ANALYSIS AND NOTES

CHAPTER I.

1. Greetings, 1, 2. Paul and Timothy, co-workers in founding Philippian church, send greetings to "all the saints," without exception. The appropriate recognition of the bishops (elders) and deacons is significant. The usual apostolic benediction of

peace from God and Christ lifts the reader at once into pure atmosphere for his spirits.

2. Thanksgiving and petition, 3-11.

a. Thanksgiving for their fellowship, 3-8. Fellowship means partnership, sharing, not only in promoting the gospel locally, but also in sending support to Paul for the same purpose. Evangelism was the common aim of Paul and the church.

b. Petition for their increasing love, 9-11. This would result from knowledge and understanding of the gospel, backed by Christian conduct.

3. Effect of his imprisonment on preaching, 12-21.

a. It gave courage to sincere gospel preachers, 13, 14. The prison guard and others knew Paul was in prison, not for crime, but for preaching Christ, still he preached. This emboldened proclaimers fearful of persecution.

b. It gave occasion to insincere preachers, 15-17. The Judaizing preachers envied Paul's success—even in "Caesar's household" (4:22). They had no good will for him, so they proclaimed a "Christ of faction," intending to glorify themselves, cp. Gal. 6:12, 13, and distress Paul. How like modern organized Christianity which demands co-operation *our way*, or else—.

c. Yet in it all Paul rejoiced, 18-21. Not in wicked motive of Judaizers but in preaching Christ, "whether in pretence or in truth." His deliverance would result from intercession by the church and aid of the Spirit, hence he would not be put to shame in his purpose to preach and live Christ. He was released from prison in A.D. 63.

4. His dilemma as to life and death, 22-26. He faced choice, not between two evils, but between two good things—to be with Christ, or to remain here to preach Christ. Rome would soon decide the issue.

5. Exhortation to a life worthy of the gospel, 27-30. It calls for united effort in its defense and propagation fearlessness before adversaries and suffering for Christ.

CHAPTER II.

1. Inducement to a life worthy of the gospel, 1-18. Exhortation in 1:27-30 is continued; four points are made:

a. Motives for action, 1-4. "If there is—"Exhortation in Christ." There is; He has made the Christian life possible.

"Consolation (incentive) of love." There is; love constrains, II Cor. 5:14.

"Fellowship of the Spirit." There is; the Spirit is given to Christians for fellowship with each other and Him, Acts 2:38; II Cor. 13-14.

"Tender mercies and compassions." There is; Christians do sympathize with and have compassion for the afflicted, cp. Col. 3:12.

Those things would complete the apostle's joy, if done in oneness of mind, love, concord, humility and unselfishness.

b. Example of Christ, 5-11. He was an unselfish, humble servant, as manifested in four stages:

"The form of God." He was nothing less than God-equal in person (Heb. 1:3) and glory (Matt. 17:2). That He surrendered to come to earth.

"The form of a servant." An actual likeness of men, hence He was born of a woman (Gal. 4:4). But He was not *merely* human; He *took* such form, "became flesh" (John 1:14), in order to serve men in humility.

"The death of the cross." This climaxed His humiliation and was voluntary, John 10:17, 18. He thus manifested His lordship, as well as obedience to the Father's will, Matt. 26:39.

The exaltation. "God highly exalted Him," made Him sit with Him in the throne, Mark 16:19; Heb. 2:9; Acts 2:36; made name "Jesus" superior to every other name in the universe in respect to adoration and obedience—all to glory of God.

c. Working out salvation, 12-18, Because Jesus has done so much to save men, 6-11, Christians should do their best:

"In fear and trembling," 12, 13; so much is at stake.

In blameless living, 14, 15. By living the gospel they are luminaries, cp. Matt. 5:14.

In proclaiming the gospel, 16. By life and proclamation Christians are comparable to lighthouse, which directs ships to safety.

Such life of faith and service was Paul's reward for labor among them, resulting in mutual joy, 16-18.

2. Paul's plan and purpose, 19-30.

a. In sending Timothy, 19-24. Information he would bring from the church would comfort Paul the prisoner who hoped shortly to come.

b. In sending Epaphroditus, 25-30. He was church messenger to Paul and bearer of this letter. Because of overwork he became dangerously sick, report of which had come to the church. Being well enough to travel, Paul sends him back that "ye may rejoice." In this case a miracle of healing was not allowed.

CHAPTER III.

1. Warning against Judaizers, 1-21.

a. Their character, 1, 2. "Finally," or furthermore, in order to have joy in the Lord warning against perverters of the gospel is repeated. They are unclean, vicious "dogs," Matt. 7:6; "evil workers" by false teaching, cp. II Cor. 11:13; "concision," or schismatics.

b. The Christian's character, 3. Different—

In circumcision. It is of the heart, not flesh, Rom. 2:28, 29.

In worship. It is directed by the Spirit, not by the law.

In boasting. We "glory in Christ," not in Moses, see John 9:28.

In reliance. "No confidence in the flesh" as to descent from Abraham or anybody else, see Matt. 3:9; John 8:33. Judaizers were destitute of all these.

c. Paul's contrast with Judaizers, 4-21. Four particulars stand out:

(1) As to fleshly confidence, 4-6. "I yet more." He was neither a proselyte nor a half-breed, but a genuine Hebrew who could boast of his religion, zeal, righteousness—a perfection not attained by his traducers.

(2) In loss for Christ, 7-11. Everything of gain in 5, 6 became utterly worthless, actually lost, when Paul chose Christ. He then exchanged law-righteousness for faith-righteousness in Christ in order to know by experience:

"Him" as Savior (cp. Isa. 53:11), friend and companion, Matt. 28:20.

"The power of his resurrection," viz., the Holy Spirit (Rom. 8:11) and hope fulfilled.

"The fellowship of his suffering," even dying for the truth, note II Cor. 4:10, 11; Col. 1:24.

This knowledge unknown to those righteous by the law.

(3) In striving to attain, 12-16. Like runner in race, Paul was unmindful of past attainments and strainingly pressed forward toward the prize, cp. Jas. 1:12. Such the Christian race to the end of the course according to the rules revealed.

(4) In the Christian walk, 17-21. Exemplified by Paul and Timothy, 1:1, and those like them. Enemies of the cross mind earthly things, are destined for perdition; Christians mind heavenly things, Col. 3:1, where is their citizenship, whence also they look for the Savior.

CHAPTER IV.

Because of 3:17-21, here is:

1. Appeal to steadfastness, 1. Pressure from enemies of the cross instant, but hope is eternal.

2. Exhortation to peace, 2, 3. Euodia and Syntyche, assisted by Paul's true yokefellow, are to be reconciled.

3. Directive to Christian disposition, 4-7.

"Rejoice," cp. 3:1. A strange note from a prisoner. Note his diary, II Cor. 11:23-33. But such is Christ to men.

"Forbearance," derived from word meaning *to yield,* or gentleness under provocation, readiness to forgive, note II Cor. 10:1; I Cor. 13:4. "The Lord is at hand" observing and ready to help.

"No anxiety." Jesus taught against anxiety, Matt. 6:25-34. Freedom from care, I Cor. 7:32, is one inviting feature of Christian life; prayer is privilege in "everything" of human need; "peace of God" the experience of His children.

4. Final admonition, 8, 9. A summons to *"think"* on standard of Christian morality, the elements of which are succinctly stated. A command to *"do"* those things as taught and exemplified by Paul their teacher and thus experience the presence of God.

5. Acknowledgment of support, 10-20. Without complaint he had learned to take things as they came. However, he commends them for sending gifts twice in his need by Epaphroditus while in Thessalonica. In return God would supply all their needs.

6. Salutation, 21, 22. It is for *"every* saint," comes from himself, the brethren with him when he wrote, all saints in Rome, in particular those of Caesar's household. To all these

Paul had told about the splendid church at Philippi. Let us advertise the church! See Rom. 1:8; 16:19.

7. Benediction, 23.

Letter to the Colossians

INTRODUCTION.

1. Time and place of writing. These coincide with the letters to Ephesians and Philippians. All were written by Paul during his first imprisonment at Rome, A.D. 61 to 63. Approximate date of his letter would be A.D. 63.

2. The church at Colossae. By whom founded is not known. The city, an important place in Phrygia, was the home of Philemon, Onesimus, Archippus and Epaphras, disciples highly spoken of by Paul whose person and teaching were well known by the church, hence the close attachment to him manifested in the epistle.

3. The purpose of the epistle. False teaching by Jewish Christians was destroying the gospel faith of the church. The Judaizers propagated a mixture of Judaism, Oriental philosophy and Christianity. In opposition Paul sets before them the majestic glory and all-sufficiency of Christ. His theme is, "Christ is all."

ANALYSIS AND NOTES

INTRODUCTION, 1:1-12.

1. Greeting, 1, 2. Paul is an apostle of Christ confirmed by the will of God. This entitles him to be heard. Timothy, a brother beloved and well known, sanctions the apostle's teaching. Those in Christ are saints and believers who enjoy the favor of God, hence highly honored.

2. Thanksgiving and prayer, 3-12. "We give thanks," 3-8. This was Paul's habitual expression of gratitude for faithful brethren, see Rom. 1:8; I Cor. 1:4; Eph. 1:16; Phil. 1:3, etc. Their lives are characterized by *faith* in Christ, *love* toward all

saints, *hope* of heaven—all of which is promoted by the gospel which everywhere is "bearing fruit and increasing." The world is getting better!

"We do not cease to pray," 9-12. Having heard of their faithfulness, Paul prays for their spiritual progress: that they may be filled with *"knowledge"* in order to walk worthily of the Lord; that they may be *"strengthened"* by the Holy Spirit unto patience and longsuffering in joy; and that they *give thanks* for being qualified for the heavenly inheritance. God's purpose in Christ is to fit men for this inheritance by making them saints in character and travelers to the heavenly country in the light of the gospel. All others are disinherited and in the dark.

PART I.
THE PREEMINENCE OF CHRIST, 1:13—2:23.

This is marked by several facts:

1. He is deliverer, 13. The word "delivered" means "to drag out of danger, to rescue," like one would rescue a drowning person. All in the kingdom of darkness are sinking into hell; Christ offers them transfer into His kingdom of light and safety through faith in and obedience to Him, so we are said to be "baptized into Christ," Gal. 3:27. And there is no condemnation to those in Him, Rom. 8:1.

2. He is redeemer, 14. Redeem means to set one free for a ransom paid. As a Roman slave was sometimes redeemed and set free, so the slave of sin is liberated by the death of Christ— "bought with a price," I Cor. 6:20; I Pet. 1:18, 19. It is that or no redemption. Now he is a grateful, free person, Rom. 6:16-18.

3. He is creator, 15-17. As such he bears the "image" of God, yes, "the *very* image of his substance," Heb. 1:3. The word "image" means impress, as from a seal on wax. That declares Him divine, the exact counterpart of God. Only such a person could create the universe and control it, for "in him all things consist," or "hold together" (marg.). Moreover, he is "the firstborn of all creation," meaning not the first created, for Himself was the creator, but He was "the firstborn from the dead," vs. 18, raised to die no more, Rom. 6:9. Others have been raised from

death but died again; Christ alone is free from the power of death, hence he could say to men, "I am the resurrection and the life," John 11:25.

4. He is head of the church, 18, 19. Christ originated and controls not only the physical world but also the new creation, the church. By Him, as the instrumental agent of God, both creations are held together. It is evident that only the creator of the church can be its lawful head and authority. That fact rules out all human authority in the church of Christ and at the same time assures her success and eternal duration. This preeminence of Christ is the Father's will, and it should call forth the admiration, adoration and obedience of all men.

5. He is peacemaker, 20-23. Only an enemy needs reconciliation. All in sin are "alienated and enemies" of God, as evidenced by their "evil works" against Him. But God has made overture of peace to them in the death of His Son, Rom. 5:8, which proves He is not their enemy but a loving Father. This is styled "the hope of the gospel," and Paul's appeal is that they be not moved away from it by the false teachers.

6. He has provided the gospel ministry, 24-29. "I was made a minister," appointed by Christ, Acts 26:16-18. Christ settles the question, Who may preach? And often it is a suffering ministry. "I fill up that which is lacking of the afflictions of Christ," writes the apostle. Christ suffered in order to originate the church, Eph. 5:25; the church goes forward through suffering in a hostile world, John 15:19. There has always been a Stalin fighting against God. Nevertheless, the gospel ministry continues to make known the mystery of God, a mystery in ages past, but now no longer a mystery, for it is revealed by the apostles as "Christ the hope of glory" for Jews and Gentiles.

7. The urgency of knowing Christ, 2:1-23. Because He is preeminent as creator, redeemer, ruler of the church and man's only hope of eternal glory, there is constant need of His teaching. This results in:

a. Concern, 1-6. "I would have you know how greatly I strive for you." His desire for the brethren is their comfort of heart, unity in love, full assurance of understanding and knowledge of the mystery of God in Christ, lest they be deluded by persuasive speech of false teachers who mixed Christianity, Judaism and Greek philosophy. The church is still in a world of the true and the false, and Paul's concern is, and ours ought to be, that she may remain rooted, and be built up, in Christ.

b. Warning, 8-15. "Take heed," be on your guard, lest you be carried away by philosophy and empty deceit of false teachers and not according to Christ, in whom dwells all the fulness of the Godhead. What a contrast between Christ and human tradition and rudimentary teaching! Traditions of men and philosophic speculations are still set against Christ and His gospel. However, these are the facts of Christ:

"In him ye are made full." He is all the fulness of God, therefore He is all one needs; human opinions and traditions are void, empty.

"In him ye were circumcised." This was done by "having been buried with him in baptism...raised with him." Then the body of sin was done away, Rom. 6:6, and the new life begun.

"In him ye were made alive" by "having forgiven us all our trespasses." In sin is eternal death; forgiveness connects a person with God, who is life.

He took away the law, all of it, by "nailing it to the cross." It was a "bond," a bill of debt against men, because they were bound to fulfill it perfectly or suffer its penalty, death. But more. Through removal of the law Christ triumphed over all satanic governments and powers who, by means of the law, had caused men to sin, see Rom. 7:7, 8, 11.

c. Exhortation, 16-23. Because Christ is the end of the law and the center of the Christian system, these admonitions follow:

"Let no one judge you," 16, 17. Then, as now, there were those who imposed upon Christians observance of the law of Moses in respect to food, drink and sacred time. These were but a shadow of good things to come, Heb. 10:1. Therefore let go of the shadow, hold on to the real substance.

"Let no man rob you," 18, 19. Since Christ is "the head of all principality and power," 10, let no one make you lose your reward by worshiping angels as mediaries, a practice in vogue. Hold fast to Christ. The counterpart today is worshiping of dead saints and the Virgin Mary.

"If ye died with Christ," 20-23. This they did in baptism, Rom. 6:3, 4, and it was a death, not only to "the rudiments of the world," "the precepts and doctrines of men," but also to sin. However, the Colossians had subjected themselves to asceticism, or self-mortification. Its source was Oriental philosophy which holds that matter is the cause of all evil. It now appears in the fasting of Lent. Such "severity to the body" is styled "will-worship," for it was imposed by the will of false teachers, but it is of no "value against indulgence of the flesh"; only Christ can keep out sin.

PART II.
THE LIFE IN CHRIST, 3:1-25.

Having been buried and raised with Christ, 2:12, it follows that our life is transferred from earth to heaven where Christ is. Note Phil. 3:20. We have ascended with Him in our reflections and conduct, and in this chapter the Christ-related life is described. It is:

1. A heavenly life. "Seek the things that are above." Cp. Matt. 6:33. Three reasons are assigned:

a. We died. Dead to the world, but alive to God, hence Paul could say Gal. 6:14. Dead to a world of material things beyond personal needs. Why? I Tim. 6:7; I John 2:17. Dead to a world of wicked, immoral men, yet living among them the Christ.

b. Our life is hid in God. He is our home, Ps. 90:1. We came to Him through Christ, John 14:6. Our life is now in Christ, Rom. 8:1; therefore, reasons the Apostle, we cannot set our mind on earthly things.

c. Christ will return, 4. He who is our life in God will come back for the rest of our person the body, and thus complete our "hope of glory," 1:27.

2. A mortifying life, 5-11. "Put to death." Death with Christ in baptism was a death to sin, Rom. 6:2. The old life cannot fellowship with Christ, therefore "your members" (hand, foot, eye, etc.) cannot be used as "instruments of unrighteousness," Rom. 6:13. On this point the teaching of Jesus is terrifying, Matt. 5:29, 30. Not a physical operation, but ethical and moral surgery is demanded. Paul enforces this by saying, "ye have put off the old man... and have put on the new." And that fact

involves, not only moral conduct, but also racial relation, cp. Gal. 3:28. Thus "Christ is all, and in all."

3. A progressive life, 12-17: "Put on." Nobody can stand still morally and spiritually. A Christian is to "press on unto perfection" in knowledge and conduct. The virtues named are held in place by the "bond," the ligature, of love. It acts like the hoops on a barrel, which hold the staves in place. To this end "the peace of Christ" is to rule, "the word of Christ" is to indwell, "the name of Christ" is to be acknowledged.

4. A family life, 3:18—4:1. What will Christ do for the home? It is clear to all that the strength of the nation and the church is measured by the character of the home. That is not a debatable question. With divine authority Paul deals with:

a. The relation of husband and wife. See also Eph. 5:22-25. "Wives, be in subjection; husbands love your wives." Only self-giving love is authority in the home, even as it is in the church, for "Christ loved the church, and gave himself up for it."

b. Parents and children. Let us be convinced that the home life will either make or mar the future life of the children. This calls for their obedience to their parents. That will go a long way in solving the problem of "juvenile delinquency." Fathers are not to "provoke" (make angry) their children by unreasonable demands, but "nurture (bring them up) in the chastening of the Lord," Eph. 6:4. In due time they will take a public stand for Christ.

c. Master and servant. "Servants" (bondslaves) hark back to Roman slavery, yet the teaching is applicable in modern life. The domestic servants render service not only to earthly masters and mistresses, but also "unto the Lord," hence are said to "adorn the doctrine of God our Savior," Titus 2:10, by honest and faithful service. The masters are to be just and fair in wages and care to their servants, knowing that they "have a Master in heaven." These principles are also applicable to the vexing problem of labor and management, and apart from Christ there is no solution.

PART III.
CLOSING MESSAGE, 4:2-18.

1. Admonition, 2-6.

a. Concerning prayer, 2-4. Prayer for themselves was to be persevering and alert as to the manner and subject matter. Note Matt. 6:7; 1 John 5:14. Thanksgiving for favors received is not to be overlooked. They were also to pray for others—"for us that God may open a door for the word." See I Cor. 16:9; II Cor. 2:12; II Thess. 3:1.

b. Concerning conduct, 5, 6. It is to be a "walk in wisdom" before non-Christians so as to avoid persecution, cp. Matt. 10:16, and at the same time exhibit the gospel in deed and speech.

2. Information, 7-9. Tychicus and Onesimus (Philemon 10) would report concerning Paul's preaching and suffering. This would strengthen the bond of understanding and sympathy.

3. Salutations, 10-15. Some of the persons named were Paul's "fellow-prisoners," others were "fellow-workers," all were "servants of Christ," spoken of elsewhere in the New Testament.

4. Directive, 16, 17. Similar conditions in the churches at Colossae and Laodicea call for exchange of letters from the apostle to them. In both churches false teachers were operating and the doctrine of Christ was needed to save the church and enable it to go forward.

5. Authentication, 18. It was Paul's practice to certify his letters, II Thess. 3:17. This would impress authority and guard against forgery. The emotional appeal, "remember my bonds," served to enforce obedience to his teaching then and now. The gospel has come to men at great human cost. Lastly, there is the apostolic benediction, wishing heaven's favor for all of God's children.

First Thessalonian Letter

INTRODUCTION.

1. Author. Authorship is claimed by Paul and never has been questioned except by unbelieving rationalistic critics. His name is still in the book, confirmed by his associates, Sylvanus and Timothy, 1:1.

2. Date and place. According to history in the book of Acts, Paul came from Philippi to Thessalonica on his second missionary tour, A.D. 50-53. From there he went to Beroea, Athens and Corinth where this letter was written about A.D. 52. It was the earliest of Paul's epistles and also the first book of the New Testament—a fact worthy of attention.

3. The church. Thessalonica, modern Salonika of Greece, was located on the Aegean Sea. Its favorable situation made it a great commercial port, populated by Greeks, Romans and Jews. There Paul planted the seed of the kingdom, an account of which is given in Acts 17:1-9. Though he was there but a short time, the effect was so great that "a great multitude" responded, and his enemies accused him of having "turned the world upside down."

4. Occasion. Terrific opposition led by the Jews caused Paul to leave "by night" for Beroea, Acts 17:10. Out of anxiety for the new converts, twice he tried to return, but he was hindered by Satan, I Thess. 2:18. When he reached Athens he sent Timothy to establish them in the faith, 3:1, 2, who returned with a cheering report, but there were some things which called for special instruction.

In design the letter appears, in the main, to be: (a) To commend them for steadfastness in the faith. In those days it meant something to become a Christian and remain such in the face of furious opposition by unbelieving Jews and Gentiles. (b) To

78

correct moral and social difficulties in the church. This condition has always obtained among believers, because they live in an imperfect world, hence need divine corrective. (c) To assure resurrection of the dead. The disciples were in trouble concerning their departed brethren. Therefore Paul gave them the plainest possible instruction respecting their resurrection at the return of Christ—words of "comfort" to all Christians in every age.

ANALYSIS AND NOTES

SALUTATION, 1:1.

Greetings from three well-known co-workers would draw immediate interest. Here is fellowship and security accorded Christians only, and only such people can experience divine grace and peace.

PART I.
COMMENDATION, 1:2—3:13.

This is called forth by the following reasons:

1. Behavior relative to the gospel, 1:2-10.

a. Thanksgiving for fruit of the gospel, 2-4.

"Work of faith." It never can exist inactive, Jas. 2:26.

"Labor of love." Wearisome labor, toil at the cost of pain, are stimulated by love for God and men.

"Patience of hope." Endurance of severe hardships is made possible by the hope laid up in heaven, Col. 1:5.

These characteristics were evidence of their "election" or choice of God.

b. Reception of the gospel, 5, 6. It came to them—

"In word." It is the only way the gospel can come to anybody. See 5:27; Mark 16:15.

"In power." The preaching was accompanied with miracles, cp. Heb. 2:4. That proved the gospel a message from heaven.

"In the Holy Spirit." Spiritual gifts were bestowed in the early church, one purpose of which was to prove that God was among them, I Cor. 14:25.

"In much assurance." By the above facts the believers were convinced of the truth of the gospel. Morever, it was evidenced by the disinterested "manner" of the preachers: money was not their motive.

For these reasons the word was received in the face of "much affliction." Evidence was overwhelming to good and honest hearts, Luke 8:15.

c. Spread of the gospel, 7-10. It was evangelism by "example" and "word." The effect of the gospel on them was talked "in every place." Cp. Rom. 1:8; II Cor. 3:2. Like all early Christians, they became messengers of the word, see Acts 8:4.

2. Character and conduct of the preachers of the gospel, 2:1-16.

a. They were bold, despite opposition, 1, 2. Recall Acts 17:5. Suffering at Philippi did not deter them. God has no use for cowards, Matt. 10:32, 33.

b. Their moral conduct was above reproach, 3-12. The gospel was "not of error"; its messengers were "approved of God" as trustees; no "words of flattery" were used to get converts; no "cloak of covetousness" was worn; no "glory of men" was obtained by claiming "authority." On the other hand, they were gentle, affectionate, self-supporting (note Phil. 4:15, 16), unblamable, treated the brethren "as a father his own children"—exhorting, encouraging, charging them to live a godly life. Here is a model for all gospel preachers.

c. Their message was received, 13-16. The result from preaching by such men was inevitable—"Ye accepted it not as the word of men . . . ." Because of this conviction, they, like other churches, suffered from their own race. What a terrifying indictment of the Jews! But the believers could not doubt the gospel. Nobody stakes his life on a lie.

3. Concern for the church, 2:17—3:13.

a. Paul purposed to revisit them, 17-20. Opposition had driven him to Beroea, Acts 17:10. While there he planned twice to visit them, but Satan hindered by sending Jews from Thessalonica, Acts 17:13. Neverthelesss the brethren are assured of being Paul's hope, joy and crown at Christ's coming.

b. Timothy is sent to establish them, 3:1-10. Because of intense opposition and suffering, the believers were in **danger** of letting go of the faith, but Timothy returned with a good report of their steadfastness which called forth thanksgiving to God.

c. Paul's prayer for them, 11-13. He prayed:

That he may visit them. His movements were entirely in the will of God.

That they may increase and abound in love. That would result in welfare for each other and lessening of opposition from without.

That they may be unblamable in holiness when Christ returns. Then there would be no charge against them at the judgment.

PART II.
EXHORTATION, 4:1-12.

In order that the Thessalonians may be blameless at the Lord's coming, they are exhorted:

1. To purity, 1-8. Immorality was common among pagans, but Christians are called to "sanctification."

2. To love, 9, 10. Affection for each other was not lacking, but they are to "abound more and more." For the Christian there is no stopping point.

3. To exemplary conduct, 11, 12. Paul laid down three good rules for life:

"Be Quiet." There was too much "tell-along." Cp. Acts 17:21.

"Do Your Own Business." Some were meddlers in other people's affairs.

"Work With Your Own Hands." That is what they were made for. In those days there were slaves.

Attention to these rules would recommend the gospel "to them that are without." Cp. Col. 4:5.

PART III.
CONSOLATION, 4:13—5:11.

1. Concerning the dead, 4:13-18. Excessive sorrow for the dead, as practiced by the heathen, is un-Christian, for (a) The dead will come back. At Christ's return God will bring the spirit from the intermediate state and the body from the grave, see Rev. 1:17, 18. This is guaranteed by the resurrection of Christ,

I Cor. 15:20, 22. (b) The living will not "precede" the dead, cp. I Cor. 15:51, 52. This is assured "by the word of the Lord," hence not a matter of opinion. (c) All to be "caught up." Christ went away in a cloud, Acts 1:9, and thus He will return for His people, who shall ever be with Him, not in the air, but in the Father's house, John 14:1-3. This is comfort for the bereaved.

2. Concerning the Lord's return, 5:1-11. To the believer it is "the blessed hope," Titus 2:13.

a. It will be sudden and unexpected, 1-3. The Thessalonians knew this "perfectly" from Paul's teaching but needed warning against false teachers, II Pet. 3:3, 4. The advent dates not only the resurrection, but also "destruction" of the ungodly, II Thess. 1:7-9.

b. Exhortation to be ready, 4-11. Two reasons are indicated: First, the brethren are not in the dark. The gospel made them "sons of light and of the day." Second, they had armor against evil. Cp. Eph. 6:10-17. "Wherefore exhort" (same word for "comfort," 4:18). The above facts will build one up in the faith.

PART IV.
ADMONITION, 5:12-24.

1. Respect for the elders, 12, 13. They are to be esteemed very highly because of their official functions: (a) They "labor" in teaching and preaching, see I Tim. 5:17. (b) They are "over you" but under "the Lord," hence called "overseers" (I Tim. 3:1, marg.). (c) They "admonish the disorderly" and may impose discipline. When elders are obeyed and loved there is peace in the church.

2. Conduct of the whole church, 14-24. This admonition is addressed to "brethren," including the elders. The exhortation contains fifteen items, each requiring careful consideration. They reveal appealing beauty of Christian character and conduct and require divine assistance, hence the prayer in vs. 23. It summarizes man's whole personality as sacred unto God:

"Spirit" (pneuma) is that "by which a human being feels, thinks, wills, decides," and is called the "inward man," II Cor. 4:16. It operates through the brain.

"Soul" (psuche) is "the vital force which animates the body," the animal life whose seat is in the blood. Gen. 9:4.

"Body" (soma), called the "outward man," II Cor. 4:16, is the seat of desires and appetites, cp. Rom. 7:18.

The prayer is not in vain, for God is faithful and will do it, vs. 24.

3. Closing words, 25-28. Simply and effectively stated, they are:

Pray for us, 25. See Rom. 15:20; Eph. 6:19; Col. 4:3. Paul was constantly facing opposition on account of the gospel, but through the help of God and His people he was confident of success.

Salute the brethren, 26. The form of greeting was an old custom in the East where it still prevails. It corresponds to the handshake in the West.

Read the epistle, 27. This was to be done by the elders "unto all the brethren" that they might know the will of the Lord. Christians are to "grow in grace and knowledge" in order to be saved, II Pet. 3:18, and attain the stature of Christ, Eph. 4:13.

Benediction, 28. As always, Paul leaves his readers in the generous favor of God through Jesus Christ. Nothing greater could be desired.

Second Thessalonian Letter

INTRODUCTION.

1. Author. Like the first letter, it bears the signature of Paul. In addition it contains allusion to the previous letter: "hold the traditions which ye were taught, whether by word, or by epistle of ours," 2:15.

2. Date. It appears that this epistle, like the first, was written from Corinth, for Timothy and Sylvanus were still with Paul, 1:1. That it was written soon after the first letter seems certain, for persecution mentioned in the first was still continued. Paul remained in Corinth "a year and six months," Acts 18:11. Since the date of the first letter was about A.D. 52, that of the second could be about A.D. 53.

3. Design. The apostle's purpose appears to have been: (a) To praise the church. Despite opposition she was growing in faith and goodness. Paul's words of appreciation and encouragement were needed, because there were difficulties from within and from without. (b) To correct false teaching. Christ's second coming, spoken of in the first letter, had become the controlling idea. The false teachers were saying that the Lord's coming was "just at hand." The effect was hysterical. Some had quit working and were living on the charity of their brethren, thereby bringing the gospel into disrepute. Paul told them plainly that before the Lord's coming there would be a great apostasy of long duration, and he commanded the idlers to work for their living.

ANALYSIS AND NOTES

SALUTATION, 1:1, 2.

The New Testament church is founded in God and the Lord

Jesus Christ hence it is subject to them alone, and from them only may peace and grace be enjoyed. Who would not be in such a church?

PART I.
ENCOURAGEMENT, 1:3-12.

1. Thanksgiving for Christian growth, 3, 4. The first letter proved a great source of strength to the church facing intense persecution. Violent opposition still continued, but faith in Christ held and increased. For this Paul gave thanks to God and boasted to other churches.

2. The justice of God, 5-10. His righteous judgment looks in two directions. First, the persecuted Christians are "counted worthy of the kingdom." See Isa. 48:10; Jas. 1:12. Second, it is just with God to "recompense affliction to them that afflict" when the Lord shall come.

3. Continual praying, 11, 12. Because Christ comes "to be glorified in his saints," vs. 10, "always" there was prayer for the Thessalonians that they may so live as to be counted "worthy of their calling" and thus glorify Christ and be glorified by Him.

PART II.
CORRECTION, 2:1-16.

This chapter contains the central purpose of the letter. It is to correct a misunderstanding of I Thess. 4:13-18.

1. Prophecy, 1-12. Before the Lord comes, three outstanding facts will transpire:

a. "The falling away." A great apostasy from the truth was often in the Apostle's eye, see I Tim. 4:1-3; II Tim. 4:3, 4. This departure will be led by "the man of sin," disclosed by history as the papal power of Rome. Paul's descriptive terms fit the pope of Rome, and him only.

b. "The one that restraineth." History records that the Roman emperors restrained the papal church in her aggressiveness for political power before the Western empire fell in A.D. 476. When Charlemagne was crowned emperor by Pope Leo III on Christmas day, A.D. 800, usurpation of temporal power by the pope was completed and the restraint ended. From that time the pope of Rome claimed authority to make and unmake kings.

c. "The lawless one." His character and conduct are delineated. He is indicted as "the son of perdition," whose activity is "the working of Satan," accompanied by "signs and lying wonders" in order to deceive. But his doom is fixed. The Lord will slay him at "his coming."

2. Thanksgiving, 13-17.

a. The motive, 13-15. In contrast with the apostasy the Thessalonians had responded to the gospel which impelled ("are bound") thanksgiving. Their salvation came about thus:

They had been chosen from the beginning, cp. Eph. 1:4; II Tim. 1:9.

They had been sanctified. Two agencies accomplished their holiness: the Holy Spirit through His word; the belief of the truth. See I Cor. 6:11; John 17:17.

They had been called by the gospel proclaimed. Now "stand fast."

b. The good wish, 16, 17. It is that Christ and God would be their comfort in affliction and their support in every good work and word.

PART III.
CONCLUSION, 3.

1. Request for prayer, 1-5. It was for swift advance of the gospel despite "unreasonable and evil men," especially the unbelieving Jews. However, the Lord is faithful, and we are confident in your obedience.

2. Precepts to be observed, 6-15. The church is to withdraw fellowship from those who would not work for their living. Recall I Thess. 4:11, 12. The command is enforced by Paul's example. The indolent are commanded to "eat their own bread."

3. Prayer, salutation and benediction, 16-18.

The prayer, 16. It is for "the Lord of peace" to be with them. Result would be peace among themselves and from unbelieving neighbors. Note Isa. 9:6.

The autographic token, 17. Paul did not write the letter but dictated it. See Rom. 16:22; I Cor. 16:21; Col. 4:18. This mark of authorship made "every epistle" genuine.

The benediction, 18. It is founded on Matt. 28:20; cp. Eph. 6:24.

First Letter to Timothy

INTRODUCTION.

1. Author. Pauline authorship is denied by modern rationalistic unbelievers, but Paul's signature is still there, supported by internal and external evidence and accepted by the church universal.

The epistle is one of four personal letters written by Paul, the other three being II Timothy, Titus and Philemon. Like Jesus, John 3, Paul took time for the individual.

2. Date. When Paul wrote this letter he had left Timothy in Ephesus and had gone into Macedonia, 1-3. This is not mentioned in Acts, which follows his career until his imprisonment at Rome, which lasted from A.D. 61 to 63, after which the epistle was written from some place in Macedonia, the probable date being A.D. 64.

3. Purpose. The letter came from a man who daily carried "anxiety for all the churches," II Cor. 11:28, and it was intended for instruction of a young evangelist in regard to his labors among the churches, hence should be carefully studied by every preacher. However, it contains instructions for elders and deacons and should be studied by them also in order that they may know their qualifications and duties. Moreover, it should be studied by the private members of the church that they may know their duties toward the preacher and officers by knowing their official duties.

4. Timothy himself. He was a native of Lystra, Acts 16:1, where he was baptized by Paul on his first evangelistic tour, I Tim. 1:2. His father was a Greek, his mother a Jewess. His mother Eunice and grandmother Lois had become Christians before him, II Tim. 1:5. From a babe he had been instructed

by these godly women in the holy Scriptures, II Tim. 3:15—the time to begin training for the ministry. As an evangelist Paul had "no man likeminded," Phil. 2:19, 20—absolutely dependable, whose whole soul was in the gospel and the church.

ANALYSIS AND NOTES

INTRODUCTION, 1:1, 2.

1. Paul's office and commission, 1. As apostle he has divine authority; as to this letter, he is under divine orders. Therefore Timothy could speak to the church at Ephesus and expect results.

2. His greeting to Timothy, 2. Conveys fatherly tenderness cp. I Cor. 4:15; utters benediction on a preacher who always needs (a) *"grace,"* because of magnitude of his work; (b) *"mercy,"* because of great responsibility and possible mistakes; (c) *"peace,"* from God in order to do his best without worry.

PART I.
TIMOTHY'S DUTY TO THE CHURCH,
1:3—3:16.

1. A reminder concerning teaching, 3-11. According to previous exhortation, Timothy is to "charge certain men" (a) what not to teach 3, 4 (anything of human source is opposed to God's dispensation of faith and causes disturbance); (b) what to teach, 5-7: "love" for God and men, from a pure heart, good conscience and sincere faith of the gospel, enforced by (c) aberrations of false teachers, 6-11 (Judaizers taught the law, instead of the gospel committed to Paul's trust).

2. Paul's personal example, 12-17. This is what Christ did for him:

"Enabled me"—by the Spirit, Phil. 4:13.

"Counted me faithful"—by trusting me with the gospel, hence must not let Him down.

"Appointing me"—an apostle to Gentiles, Acts 26:16-18.

"Obtained mercy"—when an ignorant persecutor.

"An example"—of what Christ can do for and through a man.

Therefore, "Now unto him," or Praise the Lord!

3. Exhortation and warning to Timothy himself, 18-20. He is urged (a) To war the good warfare, 18. For this he was recommended by prophets. Thus Paul and Barnabas were selected, Acts 13:1, 2. (b) To hold faith and good conscience, 19, 20. Two apostates are named and disfellowshiped, cp. I Cor. 5:5.

4. Exhortation to prayer by the church, 2:1-8.

a. Instruction regarding prayer is contained in four words: *"supplication"*—to ask for favors, same word in Rom. 10:1; *"prayers"*—to plead for deliverance, as in II Thess. 3:1, 2; *"Intercession"*—to intercede for somebody; *"thanksgiving"*—to give thanks for favors bestowed.

b. Reasons for prayers for all men: (1) The church would enjoy peace, 2. Civil authorities, knowing Christians prayed for them, would lessen persecution. (2) God would have all men saved, 3, 4. Cp. II Pet. 3:9. (3) Christ gave Himself a ransom for all, 5-7. Prayer is acceptable "in every place" by "holy" people.

5. Directions for women of the church, 9-15. (a) As to dress, 9, 10. By "modest apparel" they would be unlike pagan women. See Isa. 3:16-24. (b) As to quietness in the assembly, 11-14. Public teaching was inconsistent with subordination, enforced by order of creation, and because of transgression. Cp. I Cor. 14:34. For exceptions see I Cor. 11:5; Acts 21:8, 9; Phil. 4:3. (c) As to salvation, 15. Though ruined by temptation, she will be saved, not through *a,* but, as in the Greek, *the* childbearing—giving birth to the Redeemer, Gal. 4:4; and so shall all women be saved, if "they" continue in faith, etc.

6. Qualifications and work of elders and deacons, 3:1-13.

a. Of elders, 1-7 (bishop, from Greek, *episkopos,* meaning overseer). Because his is "a good work," his qualifications must correspond. In general they may be classified as: *moral*—"without reproach"; *mental*—"apt to teach"; *executive*—"care of the church of God." Each term catalogued demands careful study.

b. Of deacons, 8-13. Deacon (Greek, *diakonos)* means "servant, minister," is applied to males and females who serve the congregation in any capacity. Like elders, they should be dignified, of good character and spiritual attainment. For summary see Acts 6:3. The "women" in vs. 11 may mean wives of elders and deacons, or deaconesses, Rom. 16:1.

Detailed study of New Testament elders and deacons should not be omitted. Like the church at Ephesus, each local congregation had its officers—without outside interference.

7. Why Paul gave this charge, 14-16. In case of delay, Timothy would know from previous instructions how to guide the church, because: (a) It is "the pillar and ground of the truth," 15. Like pillar-support for a building, so the church is the supporting messenger of religious truth: without her the gospel gets nowhere. (b) The truth is summed up in Christ, 16. He was—

"Manifested in the flesh," John 1:14.

Justified (vindicated) of the Spirit." His resurrection by the Spirit, Rom. 1:4; 8:11, reversed the court in Jerusalem.

"Seen of angels," "messengers," is applied also to human messengers, Luke 7:27; 9:32; in this case witnesses of His resurrection, Acts 10:40, 41.

"Preached among the nations"—evangelism reported in book of Acts.

"Believed on in the world"—preaching not in vain.

"Received up in glory."—He ascended to heaven. See Luke 24:50, 51; I Pet. 3:22.

PART II.
HOW TIMOTHY WAS TO FULFILL
RESPONSIBILITY TO THE CHURCH, 4:1—6:19.

1. His duty to the truth, 4:1-16. Because of 3:14, warning is needed. There would be:

a. Falling away from the faith, 1-5. The speaker is "the Spirit"; the time is "later," or subsequent to prediction; the cause—seducing false teachers, see I John 4:1; the characteristics are those of the papal church, styled by Paul "the man of sin," II Thess. 2:3.

b. The preventative, 6-16. As "a good minister of Christ Jesus" Timothy is to "put the brethren in mind" of the above apostasy, 6, needed then and now; to "refuse" fables, 7; to "exercise"—take gymnastics in godliness, 8-11; to be "example" in character and good works, 12; to "give heed" to self-improvement for effective work, 13; to not "neglect" spiritual gift bestowed at his ordination, 14, cp. II Tim. 1:6; to be "diligent" —work hard, 15; to "take heed," 16: (1) to self—in health, habits, conduct; (2) to "teaching," lest overstepping bounds of divine revelation.

2. His duty to the church, 5:1—6:2.

a. The men, 1. When reproof is necessary, treat an old man as a father, cp. Lev. 19:32, young men as equals.

b. The women, 2. Entreat the old as mother, the young as sisters with chastity in speech and behavior. Family terms point church as "the household of God," Eph. 2:19.

c. The widows, 3-16. Two classes: (1) the old, 3-10, 16. If in need, to be supported by near of kin. Support from church is conditioned by: unwillingness or inability of relatives; certain age; good Christian character. (2) The young, 11-15. Refused because of: lack of restraint; rejection of pledge involving church work; idleness and gossip.

d. The elders, 17-25. Those devoting full time to ruling and teaching are to receive "double honor": of money, as in vs. 3; of esteem, as in I Thess. 5:13; all fairly judged if accused, 19; rebuked publicly if continue in sin, 20; carefully selected, 22-25. (23 is parenthetic.)

e. The servants, 6:1, 2. Christian slaves to honor unbelieving masters lest God and the gospel be evil spoken of; believing masters not to be despised, because they are brethren, benefited by service and beloved of God.

3. His duty to himself, 6:3-19.

a. Timothy is urged to teach the preceding and to avoid characters and conduct of false teachers, 3-10. The heretical Judaizers are proud, mentally incompetent, contentious, without the truth, whose aim is money, but whose destiny is perdition.

b. Appeal to Timothy, 11-16. In contrast with the false teachers, Timothy as "man of God" is exhorted to "flee" from the wrong; to "follow" the right; to "fight" for the faith, Jude 3, and against temptation, I Cor. 9:27; to "lay hold" on life eternal, the destiny of his confession. The charge is solemnly enforced in the presence of God and Christ.

c. A charge to the rich, 17-19. Riches are uncertain, but God is sure; wealth is for doing "good," a foundation on which to stand at the judgment.

CONCLUSION, 20, 21.

Final appeal: "guard," as a soldier, the faith; turn away from Godless, empty knowledge of those who have lost the faith.

"Grace be with you."

Second Letter to Timothy

INTRODUCTION.

This letter was written from Rome during Paul's second imprisonment. It is the last of the Apostle's writings and was probably sent to Timothy in A.D. 68, the year of Paul's death.

The epistle is devoted mostly to personal matters. Timothy is exhorted concerning his own personal faith and conduct. He is also directed in matters pertaining to the church.

ANALYSIS AND NOTES

INTRODUCTION, 1:1, 2.

1. Paul's apostleship, 1. He is sent by Christ, according to the will of God, to publish life eternal in Christ.

2. Greetings to Timothy, 2. In I Tim. 1:2, he is the "true," the genuine son in the faith, here the "beloved" son.

PART I.
THANKSGIVING AND EXHORTATION, 1:3—2:13.

1. The thanksgiving, 3-5. It was occasioned by "remembrance" of Timothy, which produced "longing" to see him, because of his "tears" most likely on occasion in Acts 14:19, 20, his home town, and because of his "unfeigned faith" transmitted to him in his home.

2. The exhortation, 1:6-18. Because of "unfeigned faith," Timothy is exhorted:

a. To "stir up the gift of God," 6, 7. Rekindle into flame the miraculous gift to prove the gospel a message from God.

b. To "be not ashamed," 8-12. Rome outlawed the gospel as despicable, hence challenge to suffer for it: (1) Because the gospel is great, 9, 10. It "saved us," Rom. 1:16; "called us," II Thess. 2:13, 14; was eternal in purpose, Eph. 1:4; is "manifested" in Christ who "abolished death" by His resurrection, Rom. 6:9; I Cor. 15:22, "brought life" (spiritual) by His shed blood, Matt. 26:28, and "immortality" for the body. (2) Because of Paul's example, 11, 12. Unashamed of the gospel in his official activity, in his suffering, in his confidence in Christ.

c. To "hold the pattern of sound words," 13, 14. Sound teaching depends on inspired words, to be guarded against false teachers.

d. To consider some men's relation to Paul, 15-18. Those who deserted him, 15; those who proved faithful, 16-18. Unlike the deserters, these were not ashamed of Paul the prisoner.

3. The appeal, 2:1-13. On account of 1:15-18, this stirring appeal concerns:

a. Conservation of the faith, 1, 2. Timothy to exercise power in preaching by use of spiritual gifts, to commit the gospel to picked men of faith and ability.

b. Propagation of the faith, 3-13. The gospel ministry is enforced by: the soldier, 3, 4—hardship and single service; the athlete, 5—law of the game, or the gospel; the husbandman, 6, 7—first toil, then fruit; the Christ, 8-13—risen, reigning, proclaimed, Paul's example, the future.

PART II.
TIMOTHY'S DUTY TO THE CHURCH AND THE TRUTH, 2:14—4:22.

1. His duty to the church, 2:14-26.

a. To "put them in remembrance," 14, 15. "These things," 8-13, had been turned by false teachers into a subversive war "about words." Timothy's corrective was "the word of truth," the only antidote for false teaching, the only remedy for a fighting church.

b. To shun ungodly teachings and teachers, 16-21. The teaching spreads like an eating ulcer; it denies the resurrection. However, the gospel foundation of the church, including resurrection, still stands, attested by divine inscriptions of assurance and duty. Cp. Num. 16:5, 26, for similar words. Duty of church is to "purge" by withdrawal of fellowship from these false teachers.

c. To qualify as the Lord's servant, 22-26. In conduct Timothy is to flee youthful lusts; to avoid untaught questions not revealed in word of God, for such gender strifes; to correct them that oppose themselves that they may escape from snare of the devil.

2. Prediction of evil days for the church, 3:1-9. It is the same apostasy as that in I Tim. 4:1-5. There the false teaching is revealed, here the corrupt moral results. It is a reversion to stark paganism, fulfilled in Roman and Greek Catholic churches who exhibit pagan religion in garb of Christianity, culminating in "the dark ages." Jonathan's Chaldee paraphrase on Ex. 7:11 holds that Jannes and Jambres were Pharaoh's chief magicians.

3. Means by which to save the church, 10-17.

a. Paul's teaching and manner of life, 10-13. Knowing this would embolden Timothy in meeting false teaching and teachers, even at cost of suffering.

b. Steadfastness in "the sacred writings," 14-17. His instructors, 1:5, plus Paul, were reliable; the Scriptures are God-inspired, profitable and all-sufficient.

4. A charge to Timothy as an evangelist, 4:1-22.

a. Content of the charge, 1-8. It is given in the impressive presence of God and Christ; "appearing" and "kingdom" are in the accusative case and convey the idea of swearing, hence the preacher is under oath to *"preach the word."* The urgency is the coming apostasy and Paul's departure—soon one preacher less.

b. Timothy requested to come, 9-18. He is to hasten for several reasons. A more touching appeal is hardly conceivable, yet through it all is the note of a courageous faith.

CONCLUSION, 19-22.

Greetings are sent to his co-laborers of former days; again Timothy is requested to hasten his coming—winter is at hand and Paul needs his "cloak," 13. Final word is an unusual double benediction of "Lord" and "grace," including his "true child in the faith" and the brethren at Ephesus ("you" is plural in the Greek).

The Letter to Titus

INTRODUCTION.

1. Author, date and place. Paul wrote the letter. Since he does not mention his bonds, it appears he was at liberty before his final imprisonment at Rome, hence the date would be about A.D. 65, according to most correct estimate.

From 3:12 it seems Nicopolis in the province of Epirus was the place of writing. There were cities by this name in Asia, Africa and Europe; but the most probable one which harmonizes with Paul's journeys is the Nicopolis in the province of Epirus on the Adriatic Sea.

2. History of Titus. He was a Greek, Gal. 2:3; converted by Paul, Titus 1:4; accompanied Paul and Barnabas from Antioch to Jerusalem for the conference on circumcision, Gal. 2:1; was Paul's messenger to Corinth concerning the offering, II Cor. 8:6; was left by Paul in Crete to set the churches in order, Titus 1:5, where he was when this epistle was written; was with Paul in Rome during his last imprisonment but left before Paul's death, II Tim. 4:10.

3. Purpose in writing. Judaizers and other false teachers were making great havoc in the churches by their heretical teaching and impure lives, 1:10-16. These Titus was to "reprove sharply," to ordain elders who were "to convict the gainsayers." All the churches in Crete were to be taught "the sound doctrine" and proper conduct of the gospel of Christ. It was, therefore, instructions to Titus the evangelist how to do this work.

ANALYSIS AND NOTES

INTRODUCTION, 1:1-4.

1. The writer, 1-3. In service Paul is God's "bondservant";

in office he is Christ's "apostle." His activity is "according to,"
or with a view to, producing *"faith,"* by preaching the gospel;
"knowledge," by teaching the gospel; *"godliness,"* by exhortation
to live the gospel—all of which is "in hope of eternal life,"
promised "before times eternal" and "intrusted" to Paul. This
enabled Titus to speak by divine authority to false teachers
in Crete.

2. Greeting to Titus, 4. He was Paul's convert by "a common
faith," a faith for everybody and for all time; was encouraged
by benediction of divine "grace" and "peace."

PART I.
WHY PAUL LEFT TITUS IN CRETE, 1:5-16.

1. To set things in order, 5. The whole island his parish;
every church his responsibility; Paul's teaching his rule of faith
and practice. Cp. Gal. 6:16; Phil. 3:16.

2. To appoint elders, 5-9. Cp. I Tim. 3:1-7. They were to be
"blameless" (a) in family life, 6, (b) in personal life, 7, 8, (c) in
teaching, 9.

3. To stop destructive teachers, 10-16. Not only Titus, but
the elders must do this (9). Verses 10-14 describe their character
and conduct, confirmed by the Greek poet Epimenides and accepted by Paul. In 15, 16, the state of their heart and conscience
is given. See Matt. 15:19, 20. What a field of labor!

PART II.
THE TEACHING TITUS WAS TO ENFORCE,
2:1—3:15.

1. Christian character in relation to the church, 2:1-15.

a. Conduct which befits sound doctrine, 1-10. "Sound" means
healthful, uncorrupted teaching, opposed to doctrine of false
teachers which had made the church mentally and morally sick.
Christians of all age levels, men and women, are enrolled as
learners. In order to be effective, Titus himself must be model
in speech and behavior.

b. Motives for such conduct, 11-14. They are: (1) **The grace
of God**, 11, 12. It has "appeared," become visible, in Christ,

John 1:14, bringing salvation, recorded for instruction of right living in three directions: *"soberly"* as to self, *"righteously"* as to fellow-man, *"godly"* in relation to God. (2) The return of Christ, 13. This also motivates right living, for He is our only "hope" of life eternal, 1:2, and He returns for judgment, Matt. 25:31 ff. (3) The death of Christ, 14. He gave Himself on our behalf that He might redeem, purify and possess us. These things Titus was to teach and enforce, backed by all authority of Christ.

2. Christian character in relation to the world, 3:1-7.

a. Duties to civil authority, 1, 2. Judaizers held that worshipers of Jehovah need not obey pagan magistrates, not so Paul, cp. Rom. 13:1-7.

b. Reasons for subjection, 3-7. First, there is recollection of the old life, 3; next, transition from the old to the new, 4-7. It is motivated by "the kindness of God," accomplished, not by man's moral goodness, but by two agencies—"washing of regeneration" (laver, bath of rebirth, or immersion into Christ) "and renewing of the Holy Spirit," that is, renewing of the human spirit by the Spirit of God. Cp. Ps. 51:10. In conversion the Spirit presents to the human mind what to do to be saved from past sins, I Pet. 1:23; Jas. 1:18; the result is *a new person.* After conversion the Spirit continually renews mind of Christian by His word, II Cor. 4:16; Eph. 4:22-24. The result is *a new life.* The final objective is "eternal life."

3. Duty of Titus concerning these things, 8-11. He is to affirm confidently, shun all that is unprofitable and maintain discipline.

CONCLUSION, 12-15.

1. Directions to Titus, 12-14. When Paul sent either Artemas or Tychicus to succeed Titus in Crete, he was to hasten to Paul at Nicopolis; Zenas and Apollos were to be set forward by supplying their needs for travel; the Cretans, who were "idle gluttons," 1:12, were to apply themselves to some honest occupation.

2. Salutations and benediction, 15. Salutations come from Paul and his fellow-workers, include all in the "faith" and exclude the false teachers. The benediction of "grace" is not for Titus alone, but for all the churches in Crete.

The Letter to Philemon

INTRODUCTION.

1. Time and place. Paul wrote this letter during his first imprisonment at Rome A.D. 61-63. That seems quite certain from the following: in vs. 22, he hopes for liberation, of which also he speaks in Phil. 2:23, 24, written during the same imprisonment; Onesimus and others had free access to him, which agrees with Acts 28:30, 31, descriptive of his condition at that time.

2. The occasion. Philemon, Paul's convert, 19, to whom this letter was addressed, lived at Colossae. Onesimus was a slave belonging to Philemon, had wronged his master in some way, 18, and had left for Rome, where he found Paul, who led him to Christ and sent him back, with this letter, to Philemon, 12. To persuade an offended master to become reconciled to a runaway slave and to set him free was the purpose of the letter.

ANALYSIS AND NOTES

SALUTATION, 1-3.

It comes from Paul, not "an apostle" as in other epistles, but one "in bonds of a chain," Gr., cp. Eph. 6:20. Purpose is to move the heart of a dear friend as he reads the request. As usual, well-known Timothy is mentioned.

Addressed with Philemon ("loving," "affectionate") are apparently members of his family (concerning Archippus see Col. 4:17) and also "the church in thy house" (in absence of church building).

1. Thanksgiving for excellent report about Philemon, 4-7. It embodied love and faith toward the Lord Jesus and all the

saints; was effectual in knowledge and every good thing; brought joy and comfort to Paul. Thus Philemon is prepared for Paul's request.

2. Intercession for Onesimus, 8-21. Intimately connected with master and slave, Paul was anxious to effect reconciliation between them and liberate the slave.

Procedure is, not by apostolic authority, but love for the aged prisoner, 9, 10; plea is that of father for son, that Onesimus ("profitable"), though once in reverse, is again profitable and returned as a part of Paul, 11, 12; was needed in Rome, but would not be retained without owner's consent lest it be a matter of necessity instead of free will, 13, 14; perhaps his running away was providential in order that he might come back, not as a slave, but a brother free in Christ, 15, 16; if he has been dishonest Paul will refund, although Philemon as Paul's convert owed him his life, 17-19; verification of sincerity in request, plea for joy and expression of confidence, 20, 21.

Here is an admirable exhibition of rare tact, delicacy, diplomacy and power of love in a peculiar difficulty—a model unsurpassed for Christian behavior under most trying circumstances.

CONCLUSION, 22-25.

Request for lodging in view of coming release, 22; greetings from associates, 23, 24, see Col. 1:7; 4:10; II Tim. 4:10; Col. 4:14; benediction, 25.

Letter to the Hebrews

INTRODUCTION.

1. Author. The letter is anonymous but generally conceded to have been written by Paul. J. W. McGarvey in *Evidences of Christianity,* Part II, pp. 119, 120, points out that external evidence "is in favor of Paul, and the internal evidence points in the same direction."

a. External evidence. Tradition of the church in the East, where the epistle was first received, is unanimous in ascribing the authorship to Paul. So did the Council of Carthage (A.D. 397) and Clement of Alexandria (A.D. 165-220), who says Paul's name was suppressed to make it more acceptable to Jewish readers. Eusebius, church historian writing about A.D. 325, ascribes it to Paul but says the church at Rome did not.

b. Internal evidence. This bears strongly on Pauline authorship. (1) Figures of speech. Compare I Cor. 9:24, 25; Gal. 2:2; 5:7; Phil. 3:13, 14; II Tim. 4:7, 8, with Heb. 12:1, 2. Paul's favorite figures were borrowed from athletics of his day, involving running and boxing. (2) Paul's view of the law. Compare Acts 13:39; Rom. 7:1-6; II Cor. 3:6-14; Gal. 3:16—4:31; Eph. 2:14-18; Col. 3:13-17, with Heb. 8:7—10:18. In all these Scriptures the apostle argues that the old covenant was removed in order to establish the new. (3) The word "mediator" is used by Paul only. Compare Gal. 3:19, 20; I Tim. 2:5, with Heb. 8:6; 9:15; 12:24. (4) Conditions in the life of Paul are like those of the writer of the Hebrew letter: (a) A prisoner in Italy. Compare Eph. 3:1; 4:1; Phil. 1:7; Col. 4:18; Philemon 9, with Heb. 13:19, 24. (b) An associate with Timothy. Compare Phil. 1:1; Col. 1:1; Philemon 1, with Heb. 13:23. (c) Asks for prayers by the brethren that he might be set free. Compare Phil. 1:19; Col. 4:3, 4, 18;

Eph. 6:18, 19, with Heb. 13:18, 19. (5) Use of the word "covenant." It is found seven times in the New Testament outside of Paul's writings. Paul used it nine times in his other writings. It is used seventeen times in Hebrews.

2. Date. At the time the letter was written the Temple at Jerusalem was still standing and its services observed, 8:4; 10:11. As the Temple was destroyed in A.D. 70, the letter must have been written before that date. In discussion of authorship, reference has been made to Paul's epistles to Ephesus, Philippi, Colossae and Philemon, written during his first imprisonment, A.D. 61-63, and it is fair to conclude that this letter was written about A.D. 63, and it seems to have been written from Italy, 13:24.

3. Persons addressed. No particular church is named, but it is clear from the contents that it was intended for Christian Jews who were in danger of apostatizing from Christianity and going back to Judaism. They were subjected to powerful arguments and severe persecution by their own race who were not Christians, 10:32-34.

4. Purpose. It appears to have been twofold: (a) to exhibit the unsurpassed glory of the new covenant in contrast with the old, and thus hold the Jewish Christians to Christ; (b) to exhort these Christians to steadfastness in Christ in the face of fierce opposition, 3:12; 4:14; 6:4-8; 10:35, 36; 13:22.

Alexander Campbell made this significant observation: "The epistles of Paul to the Romans and the Hebrews contain the most comprehensive and complete exposition of all that enters into Christian faith and worship ever spoken or written."

ANALYSIS AND NOTES

The proposition in this letter is: Christianity is superior to Judaism, as seen in its Founder and Mediator, the Christ.

PART I.
THE SUPERIORITY OF CHRIST AS FOUNDER OF CHRISTIANITY, 1:1—4:13.

I. HE IS SUPERIOR TO THE PROPHETS, 1:1-3.

1. Revelation and the prophets, 1. *"God"* the starting point,

cp. Gen. 1:1—suitable to mind of Jews. A speaking God, note Neh. 9:30; Isa. 1:2; Jer. 1:2; Ezek. 1:3; Hos. 1:1; Joel 1:1, etc.

2. Revelation and the Son of God, 2, 3. He is final speech of God—"the end"; "heir," John 3:35; 16:15; "made the worlds," cp. John 1:1-3; "effulgence" (visible glory of invisible God), John 1:18; 14:9; "very image" (exact nature of God, hence divine); "upholding" (universe operates by His will and word); "purification," cp. Rev. 1:5; "on high" (Ruler of universe), cp. Acts 2:36. *This is Jesus!*

II. HE IS SUPERIOR TO THE ANGELS, 1:4—2:18.

1. In name, 4, 5. "Son," see Matt. 26:63, 64; Mark 14:61, 62; John 10:36. "Begotten" into the world, Luke 1:35.

2. In worship, 6, 7. "Again...into the world"—from the grave, Acts 13:33; Ps. 2:7. Angels powerful, but He superior, I Pet. 3:22.

3. In universal rule, 1:8—2:4. As "God" He is honored and adored because of (a) character and creation, 8-12; (b) service by angels, 13, 14; (c) hence punishment of those who neglect God's revelation through Him, 2:1-4.

4. In recovering man's dominion of the earth, 2:5-18. (a) Original dominion, lost through sin, to be restored through Christ, 5-9, cp. Gen. 1:28. This "world to come"—the Millennial, Matt. 5:5; Rev. 11:15—guaranteed by the crowned Jesus. (b) Necessity of Jesus becoming human in order to accomplish this, 10-18. In suffering He stood the test; in death He defeated the devil; through experience He can sympathize.

III. HE IS SUPERIOR TO MOSES, 3:1—4:13.

1. Jesus and Moses compared, 3:1-6. After most impressive address to readers, Jesus is further magnified by comparison with Moses. (a) Both were faithful to God, 2. No difference on that point. (b) Jesus worthy of more glory, 3, 4. As the carpenter is superior to the house he builds, so the Christ, builder of "all things," 1:2, is superior to Moses. (c) Moses was "servant," Christ is "Son," 5, 6. Moses served in the typical Tabernacle, Num. 12:7; Christ is Son over antitype, the church, which is His house, Matt. 16:18. Moses was great, but Jesus is greater.

2. Parallels of people led by Moses and Christ, 3:7—4:13.

a. Warning and exhortation in regard to pilgrimage, 3:7-19. (1) Israel's, 7-11. Their hearts hardened by refusal to "hear his voice," cp. Ps. 95:7-11. Thus they lost God's rest for them in Canaan. (2) Christians', 12-19. Parallel to Israel, unbelief and rebellion deprive of entrance into heavenly Canaan.

b. Warning and exhortation in regard to heavenly rest, 4:1-13. This rest is set forth: (1) In promise, 1-3. Unbelieving and disobedient Israel lost not only rest in Canaan but also "his rest"— the heavenly, 3:18, cp. Ps. 95:11. This rest promised to Christians on faith in Christ, is "entered into" now, Matt. 11:28; was arranged "from the foundation of the world," cp. Eph. 1:4. (2) In type, 4-6. It includes God's rest-day, 5, cp. Gen. 2:2, which later became the Jewish Sabbath, Ex. 20:11; the land of Canaan, 5, 6, which some Israelites failed to enter, Ps. 95:11. (3) In definition, 7, 8. Through David, long time after sabbath was given and conquest of Canaan by Joshua, God spoke of "a certain day," "another day," namely, "his rest," 3:18; 4:1, cp. Ps. 95:7, 8. (4) In fulfillment, 9, 10. There "remaineth," in the future, in heaven, "a sabbath rest," literally a *cessation* from work on earth by God's people. (5) In exhortation and warning, 11-13. Based on Israel's disobedience, the sure fulfillment of God's word, the all-seeing eyes of God.

PART II.
THE SUPERIORITY OF CHRIST AS HIGH PRIEST, 4:14—10:39.

In the preceding, the Christ as Founder of Christianity has been lifted far above Old Testament prophets, the angels, and Moses. Having already introduced Him as "High Priest," 2:17; 3:1, the writer next exalts Him as Mediator above the Levitical high-priesthood in unbroken reasoning to the close of chapter ten.

I. PURPOSE OF AND FITNESS FOR THE PRIESTHOOD, 4:14—5:10.

1. The fact of Christ's priesthood stated and appeal, 4:14-16.

"Hold fast" because of His priestly greatness. "Son of God," hence superior to Aaron the type. *"Draw near"* because of His human experience. "Tempted," hence can sympathize.

2. Qualifications of the earthly high priest, 5:1-4. It was required of him: (a) to mediate, 1—a go-between God and man; (b) to sacrifice, 1—presented to God "gifts" (bloodless) and "sacrifices" (bloody) on account of sin; (c) to sympathize, 3—"bear gently" with ignorant and erring humanity, cp. Isa. 40:1. (d) to be divinely appointed, 4—must be "called of God," see Lev. 8:1-5.

3. Qualifications of Christ for the priesthood, 5:5-10. He also (a) was "called of God," 5, 6, and responded, Heb. 10:7; (b) is able to sympathize, 7, 8; 4:15; (c) by His sacrifice became "author of eternal salvation." Thus qualified, He was "named of God," nominated His High Priest.

II. NECESSITY OF GROWTH IN KNOWLEDGE AND CHARACTER IN ORDER TO SECURE THE HOPE OF THE PRIESTHOOD, 5:11—6:20.

1. Hindrances to understanding Christ's priesthood, 5:11-14. The readers were *"dull of hearing,"* i.e., sluggish, indolent, having ceased to be students of the word; they were *"without experience"* of the word in daily living, hence spiritual babes.

2. Exhortation to advancement, 6:1-3. First principles are foundational, but Christians are to reach beyond them to maturity, like Paul himself, Phil. 3:13, 14. *"Repentance"* of past sins is not to be repeated. *"Faith"* is assurance, Heb. 11:1, and some did not fully trust Christ. *"Baptisms"* (John's; in the Holy Spirit, Matt. 3:11; and Christian) had become matters of debate in the church, whereas there is but "one baptism," Eph. 4:5. *"Laying on of hands"* was done: (a) to heal the sick, Acts 4:29, 30; (b) to impart spiritual gifts, Acts 8:14-17; (c) to set apart for special work, Acts 6:6; 13:2, 3. *"Resurrection"* of all men, John 5:28, 29, and *"judgment"* whose decision will be eternal, Matt. 25:46. All the above are basic beliefs, but daily growth in Christian teaching is absolutely essential. A Christian cannot remain stationary in knowledge and still be Christian, I Pet. 2:2.

3. Terrible consequence of falling away, 6:4-8. In becoming Christians, the brethren had been *enlightened* by the gospel Eph. 5:8; had "tasted" heaven's gift of forgiveness, Rom. 6:23;

Acts 2:38; were made *"partakers"* of the Spirit, Acts 2:38; *"tasted"* the goodness of God's word, cp. Ps. 19:9, 10; experienced *"powers"* of the Millennial age guaranteed through the gospel and church, Rom. 1:16; Rev. 11:15. And yet some of them "fell away" (completed past action).

The *"impossible"* renewal of a total apostate is evidenced: (a) By denial of Jesus. Unbelieving Jews crucified Him because He claimed to be the Son of God. Apostate Christian Jews in effect said, "We have tried Christ and found Him false, a pretender and fraud, who deserved the cross," hence are said to have crucified Him "afresh." (b) By character of the gospel. It contains the Holy Spirit's proof that Jesus is the Christ of God, and there is no other evidence by which to renew the mind. (c) By the human constitution. Law of our being is: "If we do not use a faculty of mind or limb of body we will lose the use thereof." Spiritually, one becomes "past feeling," Eph. 4:18, 19. Jesus calls it "an eternal sin," Mark 3:28, 29, and John "a sin unto death," I John 5:16. (d) By illustration. As "the land" was impossible of renewal, so is the apostate—both are destined for fire.

4. Encouragement, 6:9-20. Warning is followed by confidence in regard to "things that accompany salvation," namely: *"ministry"* to saints impoverished by persecution, 10; *"diligence"* in regard to the hope through faith and patience as manifested by others, 11, 12, particularly by Abraham, 13-15; *"confirmation"* of the hope by "two immutable things"— God's promise and oath —the eternal guarantee to Christian heirs of the promise, 17, 18, cp. Gen. 22:16-18; *"anchor"* of the hope, symbolic of absolute security in Jesus against drifting (falling away, 6), 19, 20, see Col. 1:27.

III. SEVEN PROOFS OF CHRIST'S SUPERIOR PRIEST-HOOD, 7:1—10:39.

Jesus has been traced into heaven, declared a high priest after the order of Melchizedek in official dignity. Now proofs of His preeminence above the Levitical high-priesthood are submitted to the Jewish readers.

1. He is priest after a higher order than Aaron, 7:1-19.

a. As seen in Melchizedek the type, 1-3. In Gen. 14:18-20 is found his only history. Since he was both king and priest, like him Jesus is a King-Priest. Points of comparison are of special interest: (1) "Priest of God Most High"—divinely appointed first public priest over all as he was king over all. Like him, Jesus was "named of God" and for "all that obey him," 5:9, 10. (2) King of righteousness" (the meaning of his name: *Melchi* = king; *zedek* = righteousness)—that is character of Jesus, 1:8, 9. (3) "King of Salem" (Jerusalem). Salem means peace, hence a peacemaker among men. Jesus is "Prince of Peace," Isa. 9:6. His people are "peacemakers," Matt. 5:9. (4) "Without father, without mother." Thus spoke Jews, Greeks and Romans of a person whose parents were unknown. Jesus has no known spiritual parents, see John 1:1; Micah 5:2. (5) "Without genealogy" (Gr., without pedigree) —having neither ancestors nor descendants recorded. Jesus appears the same. Greek word for "genealogy" is, in Acts 8:33, translated "generation," meaning without descendants, "for his life was taken from the earth." (6) "Having neither beginning of days nor end of life." No record of Melchizedek's birth or death. Suddenly he appears and disappears in history, hence said to abide "continually." In this respect he was "made like the Son of God" whose priesthood is eternal, for "he ever liveth," vs. 25.

Thus Jesus is presented as our King-Priest, far greater than Aaron and his descendants.

b. As seen in Melchizedek's greatness in relation to Abraham, 4-10. Marks of superiority are: (1) The tithe, 4-6. Given both by Abraham and by Levi yet unborn, 9, 10, hence Melchizedek's priesthood greater than the Levitical. So Christ's priesthood is greater than the Aaronic—important for Jews to know. (2) The blessing, 7, 8. As Melchizedek blessed Abraham, cp. Gen. 14:18-20, so Jesus blesses Jews and Gentiles by deliverance from iniquity, Acts 3:26.

c. As seen in imperfection of Levitical priesthood, 11-19. It has been shown inferior to that of Melchizedek, and its ministration could not remove sin, hence need of "another priest," 11; but that necessitated change of law on which priesthood was founded, 12; moreover, the new priest is of a different tribe, 13, 14; furthermore, this priest of Melchizedek pattern derives his office, not from Jewish law, but from power of an endless life, 15-17. The conclusion, 18, 19. The law cancelled because of weakness and uselessness, cp. Rom. 8:3; the gospel followed with "a better hope."

2. He is priest made with an oath, 7:20-22. Superiority of Christ as priest is attested by irreversible oath of God, Ps. 110:4, not so the Levitical priesthood. Hence He is our "surety," bondsman, guarantee, of a better covenant.

3. He is an unchangeable priest, 7:23-25. Levitical high priests many (from Aaron to birth of Christ, 67; from His birth to destruction of Jerusalem, 81), but Jesus lives for ever, hence able to save and intercede.

4. He is a sinless priest, 7:26-28. He fits our needs because He is: *"holy"* as to character, John 8:46; *"guileless"* in dealing with men, never crafty nor crooked; *"undefiled"* in social relations by evil company—"tempted, yet without sin"; *"separated"* from men in evil purposes and plans (note II Cor. 6:17, 18); *"higher than the heavens"*—seated on the right hand of God as ruler of the universe; *"offered up,"* not daily nor for His own sins like Jewish priests, but "once for all," a priest by oath who is perfect for ever.

5. He is priest of a better covenant, 8:1-13.

a. Officiates in the "true tabernacle" of which the earthly was a type, 1-5. Thus far Christ is superior to Levitical high-priesthood, next He is exalted above the Levitical sanctuary. "The chief point" is: (1) He is on *"the throne"* of the universe, cp. 2:9— never before a priest like that; (2) He ministers in *"the true tabernacle"*—the heavenly tent, typified by the earthly.

b. Is mediator of a better covenant, 6-13, better than the old because:

(1) It contains better promises, 6. Those of the old were temporal—not one looked beyond this life. Those of the new offer forgiveness of sin, gift of the Holy Spirit, inheritance in heaven, Acts 2:38; I Pet. 1:4; I Tim. 4:8.

(2) It is faultless, 7-9. The old faulty in that when broken it had no remedy for transgression; that was its weakness. The new, predicted, Jer. 31:31-34, is superior, Rom. 8:3.

(3) It is far superior to the old, 10-12. This is it: (a) Written on the heart, 10, the old on tablets of stone, cp. II Cor. 3:3; hence the old governed from without, the new from within. (b) Knowledge of the Lord, 11. People born into the old, taught afterwards, Deut. 6:6-9. Into the new people come, first by instruction, Matt.

28:19, next by spiritual birth, John 3:3, 5. (c) Forgiveness of sin, 12. Under the old, *remembrance* of sin each year on day of atonement, Lev. 16; under the new, sins are *forgiven and forgotten.* Hear this: Luke 24:47; Acts 2:38; 3:19; 22:16—no greater announcement to men! (d) End of the old, 13, cp. Eph. 2:14-17; Col. 2:14-17. Two conflicting wills or covenants cannot be in force at the same time.

6. He is priest of a better Tabernacle, 9:1-28.

a. The old Tabernacle and its imperfect service, 1-10. The old covenant is ended, chap. 8, but as "a figure" (type), 9:9, the Tent is now delineated to illustrate Christ's High-priestly service.

It was "a sanctuary of this world" in contrast with the heavenly it prefigured. Its compartments were: (1) *"The Holy place,"* typical of the church which the Lord built, Matt. 16:18. The candlestick (lampstand), type of God's word, Ps. 119:105; table of showbread, type of the Lord's table set every first day of the week, Acts 20:7; altar of incense "before the veil," Ex. 30:6, between Holy and Most Holy, a type of prayer, Ps. 141:2; Rev. 5:8. (2) *"The Holy of holies,"* typical of heaven where Christ now officiates. The "second veil," between the two rooms, a type of Christ's crucified body, Heb. 10:19, 20, the event which opened the closed way to heaven, see Matt. 27:51; John 14:6. In this room was ark of the covenant, symbolic of God's throne, for it contained divine law; cherubim represented heavenly messengers employed for man's salvation, Heb. 1:14; mercy-seat typified God's mercy through Christ to the sinner, Titus 3:4, 5; priestly services and offerings of the old economy were ineffective, hence terminated.*

b. The superior ministry of Jesus in the Holy of holies, 11-14. What animal blood could not accomplish He did by His own blood when He entered heaven: ceremonial cleansing by blood and ashes, Num. 19:1-19, was for the flesh; Christ's blood cleanses the conscience.

c. Effectiveness of the new covenant, 15-28. Christ's death covered all sin under first covenant and after, 15; made effective new testament or will, 16, 17, illustrated by dedicatory cleansing of first covenant by blood, 18-22, cp. Ex. 24:4-8; argued by finality

---

* For complete study of Tabernacle as type, see *Shadow and Substance* by author.

of Christ's sacrifice, 23-28. If need of cleansing under first covenant, it was necessary under the second; and like high priest entered Holy of holies year by year on day of atonement with blood to put away sin by His own sacrifice. Finally, as there is for men first death, then judgment, so Christ died for sin once but will return with salvation of His people from the grave, cp. Rom. 8:23.

7. He is priest of a better sacrifice, 10:1-39. This chapter contains recapitulation and close of arguments on the priesthood.

a. The impossibility of animal sacrifices to remove sin, 1-4. The effectiveness of Christ's *"once"* offering, 9:25, 26, is proved by the law containing only "shadow" and "image" of future good things, hence its sacrifices must be repeated. Day of atonement was a backward look on sin which was cumulative. What working of individual memory!

b. The efficacious and final sacrifice of Christ, 5-10. The fact is proved by Ps. 40:6-8, which records conversation between Christ and God—subject, inadequacy of Old Testament offerings and sacrifices for sin, hence the reason for Christ's coming. For His advent God prepared His body, Luke 1:35; John 1:14. The Book (lit. *in the head of the book*—its beginning) speaks of Him, Gen. 3:15; 12:3, etc; His will was that of His Father, John 8:29, the effect of which was removal of first covenant, establishment of second and sanctification through His crucifixion.

c. Finality of Christ's priestly ministration, 11-14. Daily repetition of Jewish sacrifices offset by the "one" sacrifice of Christ, who is now "expecting," waiting subjugation of His enemies, for His one sacrifice is all-sufficient.

d. Finality of Christ's sacrifice confirmed by prophecy, 15-18. Jeremiah 31:31-34 is testimony by the Holy Spirit to the effect that under the new covenant "there is no more offering for sin."

e. Exhortation based on the priesthood of Christ, 19-39. Having such exalted High Priest as presented from 8:1 to 10:18, faithfulness to Him is urged: (1) Because of access to God, 19-25. On account of this boldness (confidence) in facts named, "let us draw near," "let us hold fast," "let us consider one another." (2) Because of terror of apostasy, 26-31. It caused infidel Jew to lose rest in Canaan and heaven (chapters 3, 4); renewal by reformation is impossible, 6:4-8; there is "no more a sacrifice for sins"—rejection of Christ is fatal. (3) Because of former suffering for Christ, 32-34. As to person, a gazingstock exhibited for derision; as to property, confiscation of possessions. It was a crime to be a Christian. (4) Because of great reward, 35-39. Boldness and patience in face of opposition would secure promise of eternal rest, 4:1; faith in Christ would save at destruction of Jerusalem. (He comes in historical events as well as in person, Matt. 16:28.) Faith will also save the soul from eternal misery in perdition.

PART III.
THE NATURE, DEVELOPMENT AND DUTIES OF FAITH, 11:1—13:25.

In 10:38, 39 faith is presented as a principle of life—"live by faith," cp. Rom. 1:17. In following chapters life by faith in Christ is illustrated and duties urged.

I. THE NATURE OF FAITH, 11:1-3.

1. Definition, 1. "Assurance" (Gr., to place under, hence a foundation of life); "conviction"—proof, as of a mathematical problem—it is *so* and cannot be otherwise, for figures do not lie: in the Bible God and Christ speak and neither can lie, Heb. 6:18; John 14:2.

2. Illustrations, 2, 3. The "elders" founded life on faith, and by evidence from God were fully convinced. "We" likewise are certain the world was originated "by the word of God," see Gen. 1:1; Ps. 33:6, 9. Without the Bible, science and philosophy flounder.

II. PROGRESSIVE HISTORY OF FAITH IN THE PATRI-ARCHAL AND MOSAIC DISPENSATIONS, 11:4-40.

Purpose of this section is: (1) to present faith as a principle of life under various conditions; (2) to show gradual development of faith preparatory to the Christian dispensation.

1. The Antediluvians, 4-7. With them it was faith in *God,* a protest against atheism. Note Gen. 4:16.

2. The Patriarchs, 8-27. Faith in *God* plus His *promises.* See

Gen. 12:1-3; 13:14-18; 17:1-8, 15, 16. They were fully assured that "God was able to perform," Rom. 4:20, 21.

3. The Israelitish nation, 28-40. Faith in *God,* His *promises* and the *coming Messiah.* Here is a most eloquent and moving record of faith's accomplishments, closing with remarks that all these people of faith from Abel to Christ had the *promise* of salvation, Christians have the *fulfillment,* and jointly they and we are made perfect through Christ.

III. THE PERFECT AND FINAL FAITH, 12:1-29.

1. Jesus the author and perfect example, 1-3. The ancient worthies are "witnesses" to power of and perseverance in faith; of Christian faith Jesus is author, perfecter, goal and example in suffering.

2. Perils threatening the life of faith, 4-17.

a.   Failure in response to chastening, 4-13. Some had become "weary" because of opposition but had not "resisted unto blood" as had Jesus and others; they had forgotten the Scriptures, Prov. 3:11, 12, a dangerous practice; chastening a sign of sonship, resulting in "holiness" and "righteousness," 7-13.

b. Falling short of the grace of God, 14-17. Evidenced by disturbing the peace, 14, 15; falling away from the faith, 16, 17, cp. Gen. 25:27-34.

3. Nature of the old covenant in contrast with the new, 18-24. By this comparison perseverance in the Christian faith is urged because of better things of the new covenant.

a. The terrors of the old, 18-24, see Ex. 19:9; 20:20. Design was that Israel may "fear" Jehovah and "believe" Moses.

b. The mercy of the new, 22-24. Christians have come to: (1) Mount Zion. Earthly Jerusalem located on Mt. Zion was type of the heavenly, Rev. 21:2, of which Christians are citizens, Phil. 3:20. (2) Innumerable hosts of angels. Christians have their ministry, Heb. 1:14. (3) The church of the firstborn. Into it people come by faith, repentance, confession, immersion, not by voting or baptism only. (4) God the judge. By faith in and obedience to Christ, John 14:6, through whom God will judge the world, Acts 17:30, 31. (5) Spirits of just men. Though departed this life, they are still members of divine family, the church. (6) Jesus the mediator. By plan of salvation, same as coming into the church, for it is His spiritual body, Eph. 1:22, 23. He is the only one through whom God deals with men, I Tim. 2:5. (7) The blood of sprinkling, cp. I Pet. 1:2; blood of Christ so called because typified by cleansing a leper, Lev. 14:1-7; is applied through "obedience" in baptism, Rom. 6:3, 4.

4. Warning, 25-29. Because of great superiority of new covenant compared with the old, warning against falling away comes from God. He warned first through Moses, now through Christ; penalty is inevitable, cp. 2:2, 3; 10:28-31. Moreover, warning is heightened by the trembling earth and heavens, Hag. 2:6, 7: first at Sinai, next at first advent of Jesus whose reign will overthrow all world powers, Rev. 11:15, but Christ's kingdom is unshakeable, Matt. 16:18; Dan. 2:44. This calls forth gratitude and acceptable service.

IV. FINAL EXHORTATION REGARDING DUTIES OF THE FAITH, 13:1-25.

1. Social duties, 1-7. (a) Love of brethren, 1-3. Expressed in hospitality to sojourners, see Gen. 18; 19:1-3; helpful sympathy for prisoners, I Cor. 12:26, 27. (b) Marriage relation, 4. Among pagans chastity in family life was ignored; polygamy and concubinage was practiced by Jews, see I Cor. 7:2. (c) Contentment, 5, 6. Never-failing God will sustain. For other reasons, see I Tim. 6:7-10, 17. (d) Departed elders, 7. Recall their instruction and manner of life.

2. Doctrine and worship, 8-16. As object of faith Jesus Christ is unchanging, so is His teaching; practice of Judaism deprives one of Christ our altar and sacrifice, cp. Gal. 5:4; Christians to share His reproach, through Him offer praise to God and do good to men, cp. Gal. 6:10.

3. Obedience to elders, 17. They are on guard over souls and held accountable to God.

4. Request for prayer, 18, 19. Ground for intercession is good conscience, honest living and a soon visit.

5. Invocation, 20, 21. It concerns (a) "The God of peace"—peace to the persecuted and distressed of the readers. (b) "The great shepherd"—leading His people. He is resurrected, hence alive, whose blood sealed an eternal covenant and who perfects the believer, cp. 6:1.

6. Exhortation, 22. The word of exhortation runs throughout the letter.

7. Information concerning Timothy, 23. The only information that he ever was a prisoner.

8. Salutation, 24.

9. Benediction, 25.

Letter of James

INTRODUCTION.

1. The author. Not the apostle James, for he was beheaded in A.D. 44, Acts 12:1, 2; the epistle appears later. Therefore the author must be the James who presided over the church in Jerusalem (Acts 15:13; Gal. 2:9), whom Paul calls "the Lord's brother," Gal. 1:19, that is, a half-brother, for Jesus was the son of Mary only.

2. The date. "The coming of the Lord is at hand," 5:8, most likely refers to His coming in the destruction of Jerusalem, A.D. 70, a judgment on the oppressive rich, hence the Christians are exhorted to be patient until that coming, vs. 7. It must therefore have been written before that event. Jamieson, Fausset and Brown in their commentary date it A.D. 60.

3. The readers. "The twelve tribes" are addressed, therefore James knew of no "lost tribes." In the dispersion the tribes were blended; those who today distinguish the ten tribes from Judah and Benjamin are *themselves* lost in thinking. Paul calls himself "an Israelite," yet "of the tribe of Benjamin," Rom. 11:1. Even the Jews themselves confess their inability to distinguish the tribes, for all their records are lost. This is a death-blow to Anglo-Israelism.

Among the New Testament letters four were written to Jewish Christians, viz., Hebrews, James, I and II Peter, note 3:1, (although all believers in Christ are included). This fact indicates how difficult it was for Jewish Christians to adjust themselves to Christianity.

4. The purpose. To strengthen the faith of Jewish Christians in the midst of life's difficulties. James knew the chief sins of his countrymen, hence he (a) warned them against their be-

116

setting sins, (b) exhorts them to endure suffering to which they were exposed, (c) demonstrates the necessity of proving faith by works. We have the same problems today, therefore this epistle is up to date.

Martin Luther imagined its teaching is against justification by faith, in that it emphasizes works, hence he refused it a place in the New Testament canon and said it was "an epistle of straw." He was against the Romish teaching of salvation by works of meritorious penance, and he erroneously thought the epistle advocates such means of salvation. But, as will be seen, James joins faith and good works.

5. The place of writing. Indications in the letter point to Palestine. "The scorching wind," 1:11, "the fountain" (spring), the "fig," "olive," "vine," 3:11, 12, are all there; "the early and latter rain," 5:7, correspond to the two rainy seasons of the country. These identification marks, taken with the fact that James lived in Jerusalem, would lead to the conclusion that this was the city from which the letter was sent forth.

6. Content. It seems to have no definite plan, yet its subject-matter can be organized after a fashion. Its forceful reasoning and profuse illustrations make it of special interest and value to the reader. He is certain to feel the power of truth.

ANALYSIS AND NOTES

SALUTATION, 1:1.

1. The author. Name and title. James, like Paul, calls himself a bondservant (doulos), hence not his own will dominates, so he speaks with divine authority, for he was an inspired man, Acts 15:28. We also should be servants of Christ, a people wholly given up to His will.

2. The persons addressed. "The twelve tribes," i.e., Christians among them, for they are addressed as "brethren," 1:2, and "beloved brethren," 1:19, etc. The term "brethren" includes all Christians of all times and places, hence it is a message to us also.

3. The greeting. The word "greeting" means "wisheth joy" (marg.) or "be joyful." There is not a sad note in the gospel, nor should there be in Christian life, cp. Acts 2:46, 47; 8:8, 39; 16:34, etc. It should always be an exuberant, zestful life.

PART I.
TEMPTATION, 1:2-27.

"Temptation" = trials of any sort.

1. Temptation as a circumstance of life, 2-11.

a. How to consider trials, 2-4. We note: First, the exhortation. "Count it all joy"—nothing but joy. The Christian is a person of faith in God, who observes the trials of His children and provides an outlet, I Cor. 10:13; hence the believer is to rejoice *in* trials, therefore there must be a value in them. What is it?

Second, the magnitude. Trials are "manifold" and of all sorts, such as sickness, death, poverty, financial reverses, persecution, false brethren—anything that might induce the Christian to let go of his faith or waver in it. These we "fall into," meaning to be entirely surrounded by. Such is the setting of life, yet "count it all joy"; that is not easy, Heb. 12:11.

Third, the purpose. Three words indicate the value of trials: *"Proving"*—putting to the proof, cp. I Pet. 1:6, 7. Thus faith is verified. Will it hold? or waver? See Abraham, Rom. 4:20. *"Patience"* (marg., "steadfastness," or endurance), Matt. 10:22. Nothing can make us quit. Job's resolution is ours, Job 27:5, 6. *"Perfect,"* the goal of life, Heb. 6:1. God Himself is the standard of attainment, Matt. 5:48. Note Phil. 3:12.

b. Difficulties in the way, 5-11. What are they?

First, lack of wisdom, 5-8. Knowledge consists of acquired facts; wisdom directs how to use knowledge. The word of God speaks of trials of life, hence necessity of knowing what it says. In order effectively to meet those trials, wisdom from God is needed and may be had for the asking in faith. Note Prov. 1:7; 4:7. In this case knowledge and wisdom of the world are helpless.

Second, poverty and wealth, 9-11. Poverty is a trial, it is so inconvenient, yet let the lowly Christian boast his high position: he is a child and heir of God, see I Pet. 2:9; 1:4.

Wealth also may become a trial, for two reasons: it is conducive to pride, whereas the Christian must be humble, Jas 4:6; it must be left behind, I Tim. 6:7. A godly man built a house, and over the door in golden letters he placed the word *"Linquenda,"* a Latin word meaning "I must leave it." Yes, and material wealth cannot stand off death: like withering grass and fading flower the rich finally fade away in their pursuit of wealth. Therefore let them rejoice when "made low." Material wealth alone is a false foundation of life.

2. Temptation explained, 12-18.

a. Its purpose, 12. It is for *approval*. It is God's method of selecting those fit for "the holy city," Isa. 48:10. Will they stand the test? They will if they understand the purpose. So the afflicted Christian woman, when commiserated on account of her suffering, could say: "When the good Lord sent me tribulation, he expected me to tribulate, didn't he?" Endurance secures the crown of life—not just a token, as in athletics, but eternal life itself, as in John 17:3; Rev. 2:10.

b. Its cause, 13-18. Not God. No evil can tempt Him, and He tempts no one. He only *permits* temptation in order to test our character. The real cause is man's "own *lust*," defined as "desire, over desire" for the unlawful which finally ends in eternal death.

That God is not the author of temptation is certain, because only the "good" and "perfect" come from Him who is unchangeable. Moreover, the new birth is wrought by Him. Three notable facts stand out: the *cause, "he,"* cp. John 1:13; the *means,* "the word of truth," see Eph. 4:24; I Pet. 1:23; "the *purpose,* "firstfruits." As according to Mosaic law the first-fruits of the grain harvest was offered unto Jehovah, so the Christian presents himself a living sacrifice unto God, Rom. 12:1.

3. How to face temptation, 19-27. Having been born again, 18, the following conduct will defeat temptation:

a. Hearing and speaking, 19-21. Swift to hear the word of God, Isa. 55:3; Matt. 11:15; slow to speak: think first. The word of God will check angry and filthy speech, therefore do two things: "put away" (the idea is as one would a filthy garment) the things named; next, "receive in gentleness the implanted word." Note Prov. 15:1. This will save the soul.

b. Hearing and doing, 22-27. Hearing alone is self-deception. It is like a man looking at himself in a mirror, but going away and forgetting. Such is the hearer but non-doer of the word of God, and he is without hope, Matt. 7:21.

The hearer and doer also looks at himself. His mirror is "the law of liberty," not the law of Moses which was "bondage," but "the word of truth," 18, "the implanted word" of the gospel, 21. It alone liberates from sin, Rom. 6:17, 18; 8:2. Unlike the non-doer, he does not leave the gospel mirror but "continueth" (Gr., keeps on looking). Such a one is blessed in his deeds. What are they?

Examples of pure religion. First, the bridled tongue. This harks back to 21. Religion without this is "vain"— absolutely worthless. Next, "visit" the needy, but not with empty hands. Temptation says, "Keep what you have to yourself." Finally, keep "unspotted" (lit., unspecked). Corruption of the world appeals for gratification, but makes speckled birds of those who yield.

PART II.
RESPECT OF PERSONS, 2:1-26.

The practice of his readers was to honor the rich and despise the poor.

1. The sin of partiality, 1-13. Its magnitude is seen in several particulars:

a. It is against Jesus Christ, 1. The Lord of (divine) glory must not be brought down to human classifications of men in respect to race, wealth, position, etc. Such distinctions sink out of sight in Christ, Gal. 3:28. "God is no respecter of persons," only of character, Acts 10:34. Christians "know no man after the flesh," II Cor. 5:16. The Lord Jesus Christ is the only way to "One World."

b. It favors the rich against the poor, 2-4. In the assembly the rich were seated "in a good place"; the poor were told to stand, or sit on the floor—"under my footstool"—a place of contempt. Thus they became judges of men, Matt. 7:1, 2, and broke the unity of the race, Acts 17:26. The same problem still troubles society, and only the gospel of Christ can solve it.

c. It dishonors the chosen of God, 5-7. The poor are His, not because they are poor, but because they are "rich in faith" (including "good works," I Tim. 6:18) and "heirs of the kingdom." But you dishonor the poor and oppose Christ by showing deference to the oppressive rich, whom God has not chosen and who are indicted on several counts.

Its application today is not far fetched. Within the church there is still need of social righteousness. Without the church there is near collapse of morals, evidenced in our own nation. The power of unprincipled wealth, greedy labor union bosses and irresponsible politics call for a day of reckoning. "Power corrupts, and absolute power corrupts absolutely."

d. It is transgression of divine law, 8-13. That law demands love for neighbor as for self, hence showing partiality breaks it; it puts men apart. By breaking a part of the law one becomes guilty of the whole; it is a *unity*. Finally, the Christian's conduct will be judged by the "law of liberty," the gospel, Rom. 2:16.

2. How the sin of partiality is corrected, 14-26. Faith alone cannot save. The Jews mistakenly believed it would, as indicated by their illegal treatment of the poor. James has already urged the necessity of hearers also being doers, 1:22. Now he argues the case. By the way, let all who now contend for salvation by faith alone hear him speak.

First, there is *lip faith:* "If a man *say* he has faith, but not works, can *that* faith save him?" The implied answer is "No."

Next, there is *work faith.* The necessity for it is enforced by:

a. A case of need, 15-17. Faith without helping the destitute "is dead in itself"—non-existent. It is not theory but practice that counts.

b. Conversation on faith and works, 18. Two persons are introduced. A says to B, "You have faith, I have works." Then A challenges B, saying: "Show me your faith." This B could not do, because faith without works is non-existent, 17. *"Show me"* is the daily demand upon the Christian.

c. Demons, 19. The Jews believed in one God. Deut. 6:4 was their creed, recited every morning and evening. Demons also believe in Him, but more—they *"shudder."* The faith alone man is not even on par with demons; they do more than believe.

d. Abraham, 20-24. He was justified, not from sin, but by test of faith and obedience. When he stood the test God could say, *"now I know,"* Gen. 22:12. What can he say of the professed believer now?

e. Rahab the harlot, 25. See Josh. 2. Three conditions would save her and her household when Jericho should be taken: (1) the scarlet line in the window, 18; (2) stay indoors, 19; (3) don't talk, 20. By faith she complied and was saved from death, 6:22, 23.

Conclusion, 26. "Faith apart from works is dead"—a corpse. Now enter the morgue. Three corpses:

A physical corpse: the spirit is absent.

A sin corpse, Eph. 2:1. He may come alive, if he believes and obeys the gospel, Col. 2:13.

A faith corpse, 26. He may live again, if he goes to work, Phil. 2:12.

PART III.
WARNING TO TEACHERS, 3:1-18.

The occasion. As indicated in 2:14, *words* had taken the place of *works*. In the assembly were many self-appointed public teachers who merely *talked,* see Matt. 23:3. This resulted in confusion and strife. Many of them were incompetent; "wise" teachers were needed, vs. 13. Cp. Acts 13:1a; Eph. 4:11.

1. The warning, 1, 2. "Be not" (Gr., become not) teachers by your own will. Let the good opinion of the church decide. The reason is "heavier judgment" because of responsibility of teachers (and preachers). "We all stumble," including James, but in the church is no so-called "academic freedom," I Cor. 4:6; I Pet. 4:11.

2. The power and peril of the tongue, 3-12. Teachers and others must talk, but the tongue can be bridled. "Let me see your tongue," says the doctor when he checks your bodily ills. So by a look at the tongue James is going to tell us about our spiritual condition, and this is what he sees:

a. It is small, but powerful, 3-6. Three illustrations point the effect of the tongue upon the "whole body."

The bridle on the horse. As a small instrument controls a large animal, so the tongue affects the whole of man's life. It has been said every man drives two horses, a white and a black: the white represents his best impulses, the black his degrading passions.

The rudder of a ship. As this small device directs the large ship according to the will of the helmsman, so the tongue, though small, determines human destiny, Matt. 12:27.

A small fire. "How much wood," or "how great a forest" (marg.), is kindled by a small fire. There were forest fires then as now, and we are familiar with the terrible results of a burning match or cigarette stub carelessly thrown away or a campfire left in a dry forest.

So the tongue, like a small fire, can destroy man's whole existence—the wheel of life—not only his own but also that of his fellow-men. And the source of this tongue-fire is hell. The noun *"Devil"* means slanderer, accuser, and he is busy in every neighborhood, and in all state and national elections.

b. It is untamable, 7, 8. Man can tame all animals, but he cannot tame the tongue, neither his own nor that of another; God is needed. It is a restless evil—always wagging—and it emits a deadly poison like a rattle-snake.

c. It is contradictory, 9-12. Its duplicity in some professed Christians is that with it the Lord God is blessed on Sunday and men are cursed from Monday to Saturday. James argues this is contradictory, as proved by nature:

The spring does not give two kinds of water.

The fig tree does not yield olives.

The grape vine does not yield figs.

Salt water does not produce sweet.

See also Matt. 12:34. With David let us pray Ps. 141:3.

3. The need of wisdom from above, 13-18. The untamable tongue can be controlled, and here is how:

First, there is a question, "Who is wise?" Paul asked a like question of the worldly wise in the church at Corinth, I Cor. 1:20. Then the challenge: *"Show"* your wisdom by a "good life." The best evidence of Christianity is to show what it can do, Matt. 7:16. It has been said, "What you are speaks so loud that I cannot hear what you say."

Next, there is warning: "lie not against the truth." A wisdom which produces "bitter jealousy and faction" belies the truth of the gospel. Now, who is a liar? Such wisdom is not from above but from below. It is characterized as:

"Earthly"—is generated in the human heart and brain.

"Sensual," meaning natural, animal like, in that it is limited to the five senses. Paul used the same word with reference to the self-proclaimed wise in the church in Corinth, I Cor. 2:14.

"Devilish": like the destructive tongue-fire, 6, its source is hell.
What a warning this is to modern so-called "religious educa-
tion!"

Finally, there is the opposite: "the wisdom that is from above."
It is:

"Pure"—not half good and half bad. "Thy word is very pure,"
Ps. 119:140.

"Peaceable"—no mental disturbance, nor social discord, see
Gal. 5:15. It destroys cannibalism in the church.

"Gentle"—forbearing, reasonable, fair. Cp. II Cor. 10:1. Christ
is irresistible.

"Easy to be entreated"—is approachable, easily persuaded in
regard to what is right.

"Merciful"—toward men in need in the way of good deeds.
The return is "mercy," Matt. 5:7.

"Without variance"—does not need to be revised; is always up
to date, hence constant, Ps. 119:89.

"Without hypocrisy": the teacher does not try to make you
believe he knows more than he does.

"Sown in peace": the wisdom from above is in "the gospel of
peace," Eph. 6:15. That message is "the seed of the kingdom."
It is sown by peacemakers, who themselves are blessed, Matt.
5:9. And it produces peace in the church and in the world.
Nothing else will.

What a contrast between the wisdom of the world and the
wisdom of God! It is divinely submitted to our choice in learning. Who shall be our teacher?

PART IV. WARS AND FIGHTINGS, 4:1–5-6.

This section is in close connection with chap. 3. It shows
further effects of human wisdom in the church in that it results
in conflicts among men, whereas righteousness can prosper only
in *peace*. In a very searching manner James discusses the question
of war and points the way to peace.

1. The cause, 1-3. "Whence come," or what the source of:

"Wars" (the Greek means "word-fighting"; English "polemics,"
which in a bad sense means controversial dispute). The Jewish
assembly had become a wrangling debating society. A verbal

war has been defined as "A war in which everyone shoots from the lip."

"*Fightings*" (the Greek means "sword-fighting," the word being related to word for sword).

These two words are not synonymous, as some think, for that would be tautology; they are specific terms, and cover the whole ground of human conflict. The Jewish Christians were guilty of both, for they not only quarreled, but also killed.

"*Lust,*" the cause of all this strife, is a consuming desire for material things to gratify sensual pleasure. Every individual and nation have this potential of war. *You lust* and have not, so you *kill*—commit murder, practice holdup. You *covet* and don't obtain, so you *fight* with sword and *quarrel* among yourselves. *You ask* and receive not, because your prayers are motivated by *lust* for *pleasures* which gratify bodily passions.

What an indictment! Is the church better today? Among her members is no *sword-fighting,* but considerable *word-fighting.*

2. Reproof, 4-6.

"*Ye adulteresses*"—"who break your marriage vow to God" (marg.) by dividing your affection with the world: this is enmity against God.

Do the *scriptures* speak in vain? No. They warn against lustful indulgence, I John 2:15-17.

Does the *Spirit* long unto envying? No. Instead of envying rich neighbors as did the Jews, this is what He does, Gal. 5:22, 23. Moreover, He gives greater grace, even as it is written, Prov. 3:34.

3. Exhortation, 7-10. Since God gives grace to the humble, 6, the following conduct will secure it:

Submit to God. This is addressed to the haughty proud, whom God resists. They cannot hope to win against Him, therefore let them submit now.

Resist the devil. Submission to God is resistance to the devil; so with Jesus, John 8:29; Matt. 4:1-11. Moreover, the devil is the ruler of this world, I John 5:19; therefore cutting friendship with the world is resisting the devil.

Draw nigh to God. The plan is for God and man to associate. To this end God chose them, II Thess. 2:13, but they had strayed. Now come back and God will meet you. But how come back?

Cleanse and purify. God is holy, hence this is required, Ps.

24:3, 4. James is addressing sinners in the church, and here is how they are to be cleansed and purified: confession of sins, I John 1:9; repentance and prayer, Acts 8:22.

Be afflicted. The Jews understood this, for on the day of atonement they were to afflict their souls by fasting and penitence, Lev. 16:29, 30. No one can recall his wicked past and feel happy. On the contrary, he is "ashamed," Rom. 6:21.

Humble yourselves—lower yourselves before the Lord in respect to pride of worldly wisdom and wealth, and He will set you on high. Cp. John 12:26.

4. Verbal hostility, 11, 12. Recall vs. 1. The speaking forbidden is of a hostile, critical and slanderous nature against a Christian brother. In doing this, the speaker sets himself as judge, not only of his brother, but also of the law (of Christ, 1:25; 2:9) and thus presumptuously usurps the authority of the lawgiver. A Christian is a doer of the law, not a judge.

5. Warning to the rich, 4:13—5:6. Their desire for wealth was the cause of war: "Ye *lust,* ye *kill* and *covet,*" 4:2, hence this final word to the war makers. So *"come now"* (A. V., "Go to now")—a summons to attention.

a. Their plan, 4:13-17. With map before them, they said: "Today or tomorrow we will go to this city and do business for a year." What was wrong in that? Not trading and getting gain, see Titus 3:14; II Thess. 3:10. Their wrong was in boastingly saying *we will* do this in face of ignorance of the future and brevity of life. They should have said *"if the Lord will."* The last words of the English Puritan, Richard Baxter, were: "Lord, *what* Thou wilt, *where* Thou wilt, and *when* Thou wilt."

b. Their disappointment, 5:1-6. (The chapter break is unfortunate; the subject in chap. 4 is continued).

(1) Their coming miseries, 1-3. Once more the rich are summoned to attention —"Come now." In the impending judgment they will lose all they have labored for.

Riches are corrupted—rotted. Some wealth can rot, such as buildings.

Garments are moth-eaten. Gorgeous garments were a form of wealth, see Josh. 7:21; II Kings 5:22.

Gold and silver are rusted. These metals will tarnish.

Like witnesses in court, these will testify against you in the last days. They had ignored the Savior's teaching in Matt. 6:19, 20.

(2) Their sins, 4-6. They are indicted on three counts:

Injustice to labor. Withholding wages was forbidden in the law, Lev. 19:13; Deut. 24:14, 15. It is still illegal.

Luxurious living. Gluttony and sensual pleasures marked their lives, despite Jesus' warning in Luke 16:19-23. They were like beasts fattened for the slaughter.

Persecution of the just. The rich controlled the courts, and thus they slew "the righteous one," like Jesus, Stephen and others, through persecuting Rome; "he doth not resist you"—Christians did not retaliate.

PART V.
CONCLUDING WORDS, 5:7-20.

1. Exhortation to the suffering, 7-11.

"Be patient." The Lord will come in judgment on the oppressive rich, "therefore" waver not, nor lose courage. Look at the former. They would not have to wait long, for the coming of the Lord in the destruction of Jerusalem was at hand, cp. Matt. 10:23.

"Murmur not." Impatience in affliction would result in irritability and grumbling against each other, therefore recall the patience of Job and the prophets, and know that the Lord is full of pity and mercy.

2. Warning against swearing, 12. "Above all things" indicates the importance of the warning. Reference is made to Matt. 5:34-37. The Jews had coined forms of profanity without the use of the name of God, just like some modern Christians whose speech is "good heavens," "gosh," "I'll be darned," etc. Chaste speech calls for salt, Col. 4:6.

3. Various instructions, 13-20.

a. To the "suffering." Any sort of trouble. Let him pray, ask for favors (present middle imperative—let him keep on praying). Note "importunity" in Luke 11:5-10.

b. To the "cheerful." Let him sing (present active imperative of *psallo*—"to strike the strings" as on a harp). Hence let him sing praise to God with or without instrument.

c. To the "sick." "Let him call for the elders of the church." They would be among those who possessed the gift of healing, I Cor. 12:9.

Prayer and oil were to be used. Thus Jesus instructed His disciples to heal, Mark 6:13; but they also cast out demons. Olive oil was much used by the Jews as a curative. James links *God, prayer* and *medicine*—just as is done today by the best of physicians.

"The prayer of faith" is classified by Paul as a spiritual gift, I Cor. 12:9, and is therefore faith in the God-given ability to heal, that is, faith in the gift of healing. For lack of this faith see Matt. 17:19, 20.

"Shall save," not the soul, but the body, for "the Lord shall raise him up" from his sickbed.

"Shall be forgiven." The connection of sin and sickness is implied, note John 5:14. Many sick people have violated God's laws of health. The conditions of forgiveness are two:

"Confess therefore your sins one to another." According to the whole letter, they had wronged each other. James called upon them to acknowledge these wrongs—a natural requirement in order to reconcilation and peace among them, cp. Matt. 5:23, 24; Luke 17:3, 4.

"Pray one for another that ye may be healed." This calls for prayer by the church in addition to prayer by the elders. The power of prayer by a righteous man is exemplified by Elijah.

d. Concerning the erring, 19, 20. Then, as now, some people were led astray from the truth by false teachers. Efforts should be made to "convert" him (meaning "to turn about"), to turn him back out of his wanderings by means of the truth, which would save the person from eternal death and cover his sins.

First Letter of Peter

INTRODUCTION.

1. Author. The letter is signed by "Peter, an apostle of Jesus Christ," 1:1, who was "a witness of the sufferings of Christ," 5:1. His importance is indicated in that when the names of all the apostles are given he heads the list. That does not signify that special authority was vested in him compared with the rest of the apostles. His primacy was in *preaching*, not in *supremacy*. Nowhere in the New Testament does he appear as head of the apostles and supreme ruler of the church, a fiction invented centuries later. Only as preacher of the gospel does he stand out among men. As such he delivered the first gospel sermon in the name of Christ on the day of Pentecost, A.D. 34, which opened the kingdom of heaven to the Jews, Acts 2. He also preached the sermon which opened the kingdom to the Gentiles, Acts 10:34-48.

2. Time and place. The exact date of the letter is not known, but from New Testament history it appears to have been written about A.D. 64. The place of writing was "Babylon," 5:13; but whether from real Babylon or from Rome figuratively called Babylon is not yet settled. In Rev. 17:5 papal Rome on the Tiber is called "Babylon the great."

3. Persons addressed. They were "the elect who are sojourners of the dispersion," composed primarily of Jewish Christians but including some Gentiles among them, cp. 2:11; 4:3. A great persecution was on under Nero in and around Rome, and it incited opposition to Christians everywhere, including five provinces of Asia Minor: Pontus, Galatia, Cappadocia, Asia and Bithynia—a district originally evangelized by Paul.

4. Purpose. It is stated by Peter in 5:12 in these words: "I

have written unto you briefly, exhorting, and testifying that this is the true grace of God: stand ye fast therein." Because of "the fiery trial" (4:12), of persecution the Christians desperately needed this epistle of exhortation to steadfastness. It was a time which tried not only their souls but also their faith.

ANALYSIS AND NOTES

SALUTATION, 1:1, 2.

It is addressed "to the elect sojourners," driven away from home by persecution, yet citizens of the heavenly home. Their election is described as:

God-planned. It was "according to the foreknowledge of God," or predetermined by Him, cp. Eph. 1:4. It was:

1. "In sanctification of the Spirit." He was the agent by means of His word, II Thess. 2:13, 14.

2. "Unto obedience and sprinkling of the blood of Christ." Heb. 10:22 tells us about this. The body is washed in baptism when also the heart is sprinkled by the cleansing blood of Christ.

Now, who are the elect? and how elected?

PART I.
THANKSGIVING FOR A LIVING HOPE, 1:3-12.

Like Paul in his epistles, Peter immediately lifts the mind of the reader in gratitude to God and then proceeds to give the reasons. This prepares for devotional reading and meditation. The reader looks at God, and God looks at him.

1. The hope described, 1:3-9.

a. It is "according to God's great *mercy*." That means the hope is undeserved by men but motivated by God's love and pity. Note Titus 3:5. Nobody is saved by his own moral deeds; it is only by God's mercy.

b. It is *begotten* (God "begat us again"): it is a born-again hope, obtained through rebirth and only thus; hence Jesus spoke John 3:5 and added "ye *must* be born anew," vs. 7.

c. It is "by the *resurrection* of Jesus Christ." That means without His resurrection there could be no hope for anybody. Now we hear Him say John 11:25; 14:19.

d. It promises "an *inheritance*." That is described as imperishable, undefiled, unfading and kept in heaven. Here is something permanent in a passing world. So we hear Jesus' urgent appeal in Matt. 6:19, 20.

e. Its inheritors are *"guarded."* They are protected by the power of God, which assures enjoyment of the promised inheritance—"a salvation ready to be revealed in the last time." But protection is conditional: it is "through faith." Only the faithful are guaranteed divine help and final salvation. The New Testament knows nothing about "Once in grace, always in grace."

f. It is *supreme joy*. "Ye greatly rejoice," and it is a joy "no one taketh away from you," said the Master, John 16:22. It would comfort them "in manifold trials" (persecutions at that time) which Peter explains as "the proof of your faith," which is more valuable than perishable gold, which must be purified by fire. And this testing of faith will result in praise, glory and honor at Christ's coming. Let us hear Paul on this in Rom. 2:7, 8.

g. It is *in Christ*. "Whom not having seen," yet you love and trust Him, and He brings to you unspeakable joy full of heavenly glory. Thus you are "receiving" continually (pres. part.) the end of your faith, "the salvation of your souls." Salvation has three phases: its beginning, Acts 2:38, 40b; its ongoing, Heb. 6:1; Phil. 2:12; its completion, Heb. 9:28; Rom. 8:23—"the redemption of our body."

2. The hope predicted, 1:10-12. Concerning this salvation, the prophets sought, searched and testified "beforehand the sufferings of Christ, and the glories that should follow them." And this testimony was intended for "you." Moreover, the same Spirit which inspired the prophets was also in the gospel proclaimers of this salvation, a subject angels long ago desired to look into (lit., stooped to examine, as illustrated by the cherubim bending over the ark of the covenant, Ex. 25:18-20). Of greater interest should it be to sinful man.

PART II.
EXHORTATIONS, 1:13—5:11.

These may be divided into three classes:

1. Christian conduct before God, 1:13—2:10. On account of what God has done, the readers are summoned to:

a. Gird up the mind, 13. A figure taken from a runner or a worker, who tucked up the garment by means of a girdle so that it would not be in the way, cp. Luke 12:35. To the Christian it means a determined effort to obtain "the grace" (favor) which will be his at Christ's coming. The eternal inheritance, vs. 4, is the object of his hope, and he must make up his mind not to lose it.

b. Be children of obedience, 14-21. The opposite are "sons of disobedience," Eph. 2:2. The Christian must not be fashioned by "former lusts" but by the holiness of God. Let him hear and heed Rom. 12:2. The demand is enforced by two reasons: (1) The judgment. You pray to God as Father who will judge men by their actions, without partiality. Therefore live in reverent fear. (2) The redemption. You were redeemed, liberated by ransom, not by perishable silver or gold, but with precious blood, even that of Christ. For this purpose God chose Him before the world was founded, and He raised Him from the dead, hence your faith and hope are centered in God.

c. Love one another, 22-25. Because you have purified your souls by obeying the truth, love one another fervently. To this end you were begotten again by the incorruptible seed which is the word of God. That word (seed) is permanent (ever living), and it was preached unto you. Here we learn that loving the brethren is a test of the new birth.

d. Put away all wickedness, 2:1-10. Having been born again, the old life is to be put away (Greek, once for all) like a dirty garment. Two reasons are given: (1) You are babes. As such you should be crying for spiritual milk (the word) to make you grow. And so you will, "if you have tasted that the Lord is gracious." (2) You are a spiritual house. This was the result of your coming to Christ, "a living stone," the "chief corner stone" of the spiritual house, in which you officiate as priests who are endowed with special privileges and honors.

2. Christian conduct before the world, 2:11—4:19. The church is an epistle of Christ, "known and read of all men," II Cor. 3:2. Therefore she is admonished to "walk in wisdom

to them that are without," Col. 4:5. The gospel was intended to walk before men.

a. In relation to civil authorities, 2:11-17. By abstaining from fleshly lusts, the heathen about you may be led to glorify God when they see your good conduct, cp. Matt. 5:16. Therefore "be subject to every ordinance of man for the Lord's sake." And never use your Christian freedom as an excuse for doing wickedness: you are "bondservants of God." Chrysostom said, "No one can harm a man who does not harm himself."

b. In relation to the family, 2:18—3:7. It is impressive to note in the apostolic writings the careful attention to family life. It affects not only the power of the church but also the destiny of the state.

Servants, 18-25. Complete subjection in obedience to masters is demanded, even though treated unjustly. Christ is the example. When He was insulted He did not threaten revenge but committed Himself to the righteous Judge. He even "bore our sins in his own body upon the tree," which resulted not only in our death to sin, but also in our spiritual healing.

Wives, 3:1-6. Submission to their husbands is enjoined, so that by Christian conduct the unbelieving husband may be led to God. Their real beauty should not be outward tinsel but inward character of a meek and quiet spirit.

Husbands, 7. They are to regulate the home life according to knowledge and understanding. "Honor" is due the wife, because both are joint-heirs of eternal life. Neglect will affect prayer.

c. In relation to persecution, 3:8—4:6.

(1) How to face a hostile world, 8-17.

Right living among themselves prepares for right conduct towards opposers, 8.

Enemies of the faith are not to be retaliated, 9-12. The impelling reason is "the eyes of the Lord are upon the righteous," but His face "is upon them that do evil."

No harm will come to those who do good, 13. Cp. Gal. 5:22, 23, "against such there is no law," pagan or civil. That is why the gospel can go anywhere and win respect. However, if suffering should come, set Christ in the heart and be ready to give a reason for your hope, 14-17.

(2) Christ the partner in suffering, 18-22. The Christian suffers side by side with the suffering Christ. His body was put to death but made alive in (or by) the Spirit, cp. Rom. 8:11.

In (or by) the same Spirit He preached through Noah to the Antediluvians, see II Pet. 2:5. The reason stated is "that they might be judged according to men in the flesh," 4:6. There is no post-mortem gospel, and, if there were, why limit it to the Antediluvians? That people was in a figurative prison for "a hundred and twenty years" (Gen. 6:3), shut up unto obedience or disobedience.

Noah and family were saved through water, dative of means: it bore up the ark; likewise the same means, "even baptism," saves people now; and it is "an appeal to God for a clear conscience" (R.S.V.) through the resurrected and reigning Christ, by whom we come to God, John 14:6.

(3) Armed for suffering, 4:1-6. Christ suffered in the flesh "for sins," 3:18; "he died unto sin," Rom. 6:10. "Arm ye yourselves also with the same mind," "reckon ye also yourselves to be dead unto sin," Rom. 6:11.

"He that hath suffered in the flesh" on account of his faith, "if the will of God should so will," 3:17, that one "hath ceased from sin" and no longer lives the sinful life he once lived. This seems strange to former associates who shall give account to the Judge of all men. Because of this, the gospel was preached to those who died "in the days of Noah," 3:19, 20, so that they might be judged according to their conduct while "in the flesh" and also give them opportunity of life eternal. This they refused.

3. Christian conduct in the church, 4:7—5:11. This last division in the series of exhortations is urged upon the brethren for the following reasons:

a. The end of all things is near, 4:7-11. What end? Not the end of the world, for it still continues, but most likely it looks forward to the destruction of Jerusalem and the end of the Mosaic institution. The epistle was addressed to Christian Jews in dispersion, persecuted not only by Rome but also by their own race. "Therefore," because of the impending judgment, the believers are exhorted concerning:

Prayer, 7. Divine help is needed.

Mutual love, 8. This will cover a multitude of sins: "Love suffereth long, and is kind."

Hospitality, 9. Christians were driven from place to place; the gospel preacher had no parsonage.

Spiritual gifts, 10, 11. They had a threefold purpose: to reveal the gospel; to confirm the gospel; and to guide the church until the gospel was fully revealed. In I Cor. 12, 13, 14, Paul presents a full discussion of these gifts. Peter directs possessors of these gifts to use them properly "as good stewards of the manifold grace of God" and to His glory. Although these gifts are not in the church now, we have the gospel they revealed.

b. "The fiery trials," 4:12-19. Three main thoughts appear:

First, the purpose of persecution. Figuratively it is called "fiery trials," implying refining effect upon faith. See Isa. 48:10. The purpose is "to prove you," to test them whether they were "worthy of the kingdom," II Thess. 1:5. However, in some cases this was more than a figure of speech. Nero had Christians smeared with combustibles, tied to stakes and set on fire to illuminate his gardens at night.

Second, the attitude in persecution. In this experience they are "partakers of Christ's sufferings," sharing with Him, hence "rejoice." Moreover, there will be joy in sharing Christ's glory, Col. 3:4. But let them take care not to suffer as evil-doers. On the other hand, it is no disgrace to suffer as a Christian; "let him glorify God in this name."

Third, the judgment of persecution. It is in process now in the form of fiery trials to the Christians; and if they are not exempt, "what shall be the end of them that obey not the gospel of God?" The answer is in II Thess. 1:7-9.

c. The shepherds and the flock, 5:1-11.

The elders of the church are addressed by Peter as a "fellow-elder," one not above them, but an equal, who actually saw Christ suffer. That qualified him an apostle and gave weight to his exhortation. Their duty is to "tend the flock of God." The Greek for "tend" means to act like a shepherd who leads, feeds and protects the sheep. This service is to be rendered "willingly," not as over-lords, but as "ensamples" of Christian living. By so doing they will be crowned by the Chief Shepherd.

The rest of the members are not overlooked. The younger

are to submit to the older, and all are to serve one another in humility under God, who will exalt them in due time and who constantly cares for them. Warning against the devil is needed, for there really is such a personality, who, like "a roaring lion," is always about looking for prey. But he can be defeated by steadfastness in the faith and God's help.

CONCLUDING WORDS, 12-14.

Sylvanus, a "faithful brother," was the bearer of the letter.

The purpose of writing was to testify "the true grace of God" and to urge steadfastness therein. Now Peter seems to recall the Savior's word, Luke 22:32b.

The greetings are from the church in Babylon (recall Introduction, div. 2) and from Mark (see Acts 15:37-40). He has changed, II Tim. 4:11.

The benediction of "peace" was used by Christ, John 14:27, and His apostles. It means unity and harmony in the church and is a fruit of the Holy Spirit, Gal. 5:22.

Second Letter of Peter

INTRODUCTION.

1. The author. Some critics have denied Peter the authorship, but internal evidence is conclusive. The epistle was written in the name of "Simon Peter, a servant and apostle of Jesus Christ." 1:1. There is no evidence which proves that a forgery. The writer was with the Lord at His transfiguration, 1:18. Matt. 17:1; Mark 9:2; Luke 9:28 testify that he was present on that occasion. That, too, confirms genuineness of authorship. Furthermore, the author had written a former epistle to the same people, 3:1. That means the two letters share the same fate. If the second is a forgery, so is the first.

2. Time and place. Peter speaks of his swiftly approaching death, 1:14. The exact time of his death is unknown, but the early church Fathers state in their writings that he was crucified about the same time Paul was put to death under Nero, which took place in A.D. 68. The approximate date for the letter would be about A.D. 67. The place of writing is not known.

3. Purpose. The design of the first epistle was to urge steadfastness in the faith in the face of terrifying persecution. The second letter deals with a new problem in the churches. The occasion and purpose are set forth in 3:17, 18. Two points are stressed: (1) The errors of false teachers. They are extremely immoral in conduct (Chap. 2), and they deny the return of Christ (Chap. 3). These are to be guarded against. (2) The necessity of growth in grace and knowledge lest they be led astray. Their only safety is in the knowledge and power of Christ.

ANALYSIS AND NOTES

INTRODUCTION, 1:1, 2.

1. The writer. He gives his name and then proceeds to state his relation to Christ. His personal relation is that of "servant," meaning in those days a bondslave, an accurate term for Christians then and now. His official relation is that of an "apostle," meaning one sent forth, see John 20:21. That office is now vacant in the church, despite the claim of some; the gospel is fully revealed.

2. The persons addressed. They shared with the apostle "a like precious faith." In those days there was but "one faith" and the one Book; and its effect was and is "the righteousness of our God," that is, the God-righteousness, cp. Rom. 1:17. Since it is "precious" (very valuable) who would not want it?

3. The greeting. The benediction of "grace [favor] and peace" to the believer will multiply through knowledge of God and Christ, an incentive to study God's word.

PART I.
EXHORTATION TO CHRISTIAN PROGRESS, 1:3-21.

1. Introductory statement, 3, 4. Its basic thought is the all-comprehensive gift. It consists of everything pertaining to "life and godliness."

It has come to us through "divine power," the Holy Spirit who inspired the apostles to reveal the gospel.

The medium through which the gift is communicated is God's call: "he called us," cp. II Thess. 2:14. The call is sounded wherever the gospel is proclaimed.

The call grants God's "precious and exceeding great promises." Precious in effect—satisfying the heart; great in extent—covering all man's needs; productive of character—men become "partakers of the divine nature" and thus escape "the corruption that is in the world by lust." The inevitable choice must be between the character of God and that of a corrupt world.

2. The highway to heaven, 5-11. "For this very cause" or reason, namely, the complete gift of God in Christ as stated above, conditional efforts are required for "entrance into the eternal kingdom" (vs. 11). "All diligence" is to be added to what God has done.

a. Specific directions, 5-7. Eight requisites mark the way to the Holy City, and the traveler can know at any time where he is and how far yet to go. Isa. 35:8 speaks of "a highway" called "the way of holiness," and this is it.

Faith is the starting point and the foundation for what follows. In Heb. 11:1 "faith is assurance." The Greek for "assurance" means "set under," like a foundation for a house. Hence faith in Christ is the foundation on which the believer stands, and from there on he takes steps heavenward, as follows:

Virtue, from Latin *virtus,* meaning "strength, courage." In the days of the Roman empire it was manifested in courage and honor of the citizen. Courage, enforced by divine strength, must characterize the Christian. He faces a hostile world, but note John 16:33. Like all the terms which follow, virtue is the result of faith.

Knowledge. What kind? Secular, yes, but more. Prov. 1:7 names the starting point. It includes information regarding God and Christ with reference to eternal life, John 17:3. The Bible is the student's complete textbook, full of supernatural knowledge, II Tim. 3:16, 17.

Self-control. It involves the mind, Phil. 4:8—"think on these things"; and it checks the body, I Cor. 9:27—"bring it into bondage" in regard to unlawful desires and their gratification.

Patience. From a word meaning "steadfastness, endurance." Its design is to meet opposition and the hardships of life. Jesus used the word in foretelling persecution against His apostles, saying, "in your patience ye shall win your souls," Luke 21:19. The good-ground Christian brings forth fruit "with patience," Luke 8:15. Trials of various magnitudes will come, "but he that endures to the end, the same shall be saved," Matt. 24:13. Faith never wavers.

Godliness. It means "reverential feeling, devotion" which indicates one's attitude toward God (a) in worship—it calls for approach to Him "in reverence and awe," not in frivolity and thoughtlessness; (b) in character and conduct: here God-likeness means being and acting like God; He is helpful and holy.

Brotherly kindness. The Greek anglicized is *Philadelphia* and is applied to *Christian* brethren. I Pet. 1:22 summarizes it. It results from a cleansed heart, is genuine and fervent.

Love. A different word from the preceding brotherly love. Is manifest in well-wishing and benevolence and is to be extended to all men without distinction, I Thess. 5:12; Gal. 6:10.

b. Importance of action, 8-11. The way of holiness has been marked; next, the traveler must make the waymarks the part of his conduct.

If he does, he will be active and fruitful, because he knows Jesus Christ. His purpose is Phil. 1:21a.

If he doesn't, disaster will follow: he will be near-sighted, seeing only the things of this world, forgetful of his baptism which cleansed him from his old sins.

"Wherefore" the more diligence is required in order to make the calling and election "sure." This will prevent stumbling and assure entrance into heaven.

c. Necessity of repetition, 12-21. The reasons assigned are:

Christians forget, hence need to be reminded (to be put "in remembrance"). How true! Is still needed.

Death is near ("cometh swiftly"), a death Christ had predicted, John 21:18, 19. Hence Peter would make the most of his remaining time. His last thought was concern for the church.

Christ is no myth. Peter's proclamation of Him was not made up of "cunningly devised fables," for he saw Christ's glory and heard God's voice concerning Him "in the holy mount." Evidence of Christ is still needed.

Testimony of the prophets is verified. When God said, "This is my beloved Son," what the prophets had said of Him was made "more sure." He was the Messiah foretold. Their word should be heeded, because it is like a lamp "in a dark place," and it did not come by impulse of man's will but was spoken by men "moved by the Holy Spirit."

PART II.
WARNING AGAINST FALSE TEACHERS, 2:1-22.

This chapter is a transition from the true prophets in chap.

1 to the false prophets. The early church was harassed by persecution from without and by the false from within. There were "false prophets," "false apostles" and "false brethren," II Cor. 11:13, 26. In the face of all this the church has survived through the centuries, which positively proves her a divine institution. Jesus warned against "false prophets," Matt. 7:15, and now Peter in violent language is exposing them.

1. Prediction of their coming and punishment, 1-9. As there were false prophets in Israel, so there would be in the church. These heretical teachers would deny "the Master that bought them." Many would follow their teaching and thereby discredit "the way of truth." Parallel to them are those in the church now who deny the virgin birth of Christ. Many departures from the way of truth are before our eyes.

But their downfall is certain. God did not spare angels who sinned, neither the ancient world except Noah, nor Sodom and Gomorrah except Lot. Therefore the Lord can deliver the godly and keep the unrighteous for punishment.

2. Description of their character and conduct, 10-22. It is a terrible indictment of their sensuality, lawlessness and corruption which they by teaching and example promulgated. It seems unthinkable to the modern reader that such abominable teachers and followers would be tolerated in the church. Jesus drew the line in his prayer for His disciples in John 17, saying, "these are in the world . . . . but not of the world." That must be the constant thought and practice of the church.

In vss. 20-22, the apostle has this word concerning these deserters of the Christ. He affirms that ignorance of the way of righteousness is better than, after knowing it, "to turn back from the holy commandment." They enact the proverbs about the "dog returning to his vomit" and "the sow that had washed to wallow in the mire."

PART III.
DENIAL AND DEFENSE OF CHRIST'S RETURN, 3:1-18.

1. A reminder to believers, 1-3. The purpose in writing was to "stir up," to rouse, the readers in regard to what prophets and

apostles had predicted concerning the coming apostasy. Then and now the word of God will protect the believer and convict the gainsayer.

2. The derisive speech of scoffers, 4. Scornfully they ask, "Where is the promise of his coming?" Their reasoning is there has been no change since beginning of creation, therefore the promise of Christ's return is incredible. In attitude they are like Lot's sons-in-law, Gen. 19:14, and apostate Israel, Isa. 5:19.

3. Refutation of the scoffers, 5-7. They "wilfully [purposely] forget" the power and certainty of the word of God in relation to three facts: (a) the origin of the universe, cp. Ps. 33:9; (b) the flood, see Gen. 6:13; 7:11; (c) the dissolution of the heavens and earth by fire. These are stored with fire and the word of God is the match that will set off this mighty conflagration in the day of judgment of ungodly men. The conclusion is that the word of God in regard to Christ's return is absolutely reliable.

4. Delay of His coming 8, 9. Two reasons for delay are given: (a) The difference between God and men in counting time. God will keep His promise according to His own calendar, not men's. Cp. Ps. 90:4. (b) The love and mercy of God. His wish is that all may come to repentance. Note Isa. 30:18; Ezek. 18:23.

5. Description of His coming, 10-13. Though delayed, the day of the Lord will come. It is marked by certain characteristics:

It will be unexpected—"as a thief"—hence readiness is urged, Matt. 24:43, 44.

It will be catastrophic. Heavens and earth "shall pass away with a great noise"—Greek, "with rushing swiftness." Then will be dissolved with fervent heat, not only the heavens, but also the earth with all its works of God and man. Additional particulars are given in Matt. 24:29, 30. The light of sun and moon shall go out, the stars shall fall, the powers of heaven shall be shaken, and then shall Christ appear. Let the modern astronomer turn his telescope on this.

It raises a question. In view of these certain events, "what manner of persons ought ye to be?"—the implication being *right now!* The answer is "holy living, godliness, and earnestly desiring the coming day of God." Then there will be new heavens and earth characterized by "righteousness." Not iniquity, but righteousness shall finally triumph. Note Isa. 65:17; Rev. 21:1.

6. Exhortations based on His coming, 14-18. Because of Christ's return, the brethren are urged to live a peaceful, clean and blameless life. Cp. I Cor. 1:8; Phil. 1:10; I Thess. 5:23.

The reason for the Lord's waiting is men's salvation (vs. 9), a fact also stated by Paul in his writing to them—not an epistle now lost, but letters written to the same circle of readers addressed by Peter (see I Pet. 1:1). Hence in Gal. 1:7 Paul warns against those who "would pervert the gospel of Christ"; in Eph. 4:30 it is "the day of redemption"; in Col. 3:4 "Christ shall be manifested." In all of his epistles Paul speaks of "these things" to come. Some of his language is hard to understand, which the ignorant and unsteadfast distort to their own destruction.

Having been forewarned, the brethren are to beware of false teachers lest they lose their steadfastness. Recall 2:18. On the contrary they are to grow in the favor and knowledge of Christ, cp. Eph. 4:15; I Pet. 2:2. "To him be the glory now" and "unto the day of eternity" (margin), that is, the day when time ends and eternity begins, the end of the world and the coming of Christ, Matt. 24:3.

First Letter of John

INTRODUCTION.

1. Author. The three epistles ascribed to John were written without name of author, as was also the Gospel of John, but the first paragraph of the first epistle clearly indicates it was written by an apostle. The writer bears testimony to that which he had "heard, seen, and handled concerning the Word of life." That is definitely apostolic testimony. Identity of style and diction in the three epistles and the fourth Gospel indicate that all of them came from the same author. This agrees with the testimony of early Christian writers, and it is accepted by the majority of modern Bible scholars.

2. Time and place. The three epistles were written nearly at the same time, and about A.D. 90. It is generally admitted that they were written from Ephesus where John resided and exercised oversight of the churches in and near that place. He seems to have been very old when he wrote, for he addresses young and old as "Little children," "my little children." From this it is concluded that the epistles were among the last of the New Testament books.

3. Persons addressed. The first epistle is not addressed to any particular church or individual, and therefore it is a general communication to all Christians wherever they may be found. That makes it of special interest to the church of today.

4. Purpose. It is stated in 1:1-4. It is to declare "the Word of life," the Christ, in order that the writer and reader may together have fellowship with God and Christ and thus experience the fullest joy. At the same time the proposition draws distinction between the *"world"* and *"believers."* Those of the world are "children of the devil"; the believers are "children of **God**."

144

ANALYSIS AND NOTES

The topical arrangement is quite complicated, for subjects are stated and re-stated, hence a strictly logical analysis is impossible, only the main points can be indicated. However, the teaching is simply stated and clearly applied.

INTRODUCTION, 1:1-4.

1. The subject. It "was from the beginning," is defined as "the Word of life." John 1:1 reads "in the beginning," and the subject is called "the Word." In both records John speaks of the same subject, namely, Christ Himself, who was with God and was God. John has no other subject to write about. He is the preacher's only message, I Cor. 2:2.

2. The evidence. It is not a matter of opinion. Christ was "manifested" and "we have heard, seen, and handled" Him while He lived and after His resurrection, see Luke 24:39; Acts 4:20. That is acceptable evidence in any court in the world. No informed person can honestly deny the fact of Christ.

3. The purpose. These facts we "declare" and "write" for two reasons: *"fellowship,"* human and divine cp. I Cor. 1:9; *"joy,"* complete in Christ, note Phil. 4:4.

PART I.
CONDITIONS OF THE FELLOWSHIP, 1:5—2:29.

There can be no fellowship with God and indifference to sin. The conditions require:

1. A walk in the light, 1:5-10. The God of fellowship is *"Light,"* hence for a Christian to live in darkness would be telling and living a lie; he has lost his way, John 12:25.

But a life in God's light means fellowship not only with God but also with one another, and there is cleansing from sin by the blood of Jesus—provided we confess our sins, cp. Acts 8:22; Prov. 28:13.

If we claim sinless perfection we deceive ourselves, make God a liar, and His word is not in us.

2. A life of obedience, 2:1-6. The purpose in writing is to

help the Christian avoid sin. But if he should sin, he has in Jesus an *"Advocate"*—intercessor, Heb. 7:25, also *"propitiation,"* a word for "mercy-seat," Heb. 9:5, the cover for the ark. Christ is the cover for everybody's sins: His blood puts them out of sight, Rom. 3:25.

The condition for retaining this experimental knowledge of God is that "we keep his commandments," otherwise we lie. Our pattern of life is Christ Himself, vs. 6, cp. II Pet. 2:21, where "pattern" means "a writing-copy," hence we are to live Him, Phil. 1:21.

3. A life of affection, 7-11. The old commandment is "love one another," I John 3:11; the new commandment is "love one another, *even as I have loved you,"* John 13:34. That means love is proved by benevolent deeds. He laid down His life. By such love "the darkness is passing away," and brotherly love or the lack of it indicates whether one is in the light or the dark. "God is light."

4. An unworldly life, 12-17. The epistle is addressed to disciples of all ages and character, divided into three classes: (a) "little children," or new converts, who had been "forgiven"; (b) "fathers," or those older in the faith, who have known Christ "who is from the beginning"; (c) "young men," or younger Christians who "have overcome [vigorously] the evil one."

Having secured attention of those addressed, the precept is, "love not the world." The Greek for world is *kósmos,* meaning: (a) the world of men, John 15:19, who are governed by "lust"; (b) the world of "things." These cannot be loved for two reasons: Love for God and love for the world cannot exist at the same time, cp. II Tim. 4:10; Matt. 6:24. Furthermore, the world of wicked men and material things will perish; only he who does the will of God lives for ever.

5. A resistance to antichrist, 18-29. "Antichrist" means one "against Christ, an opposer of Christ" by impersonation, or teaching, or both. In early days his appearance marked "the last hour" of the Jewish state just before destruction of Jerusalem, as foretold by Christ, Matt. 24:5.

"Many antichrists" were in the early church, but "'went out.'" Now they are permitted to stay in the church while they deny the virgin birth of Christ and teach communism, a system anti-God and anti-Christ.

The early church was protected against false teachers by "an anointing from the Holy One," a spiritual gift called "discerning of spirits," I Cor. 12:10. Though not in the church now, she has the complete gospel by which to distinguish between a lie and the truth.

The appeal is to stay within the truth concerning Christ and thus retain fellowship of the Son and the Father and insure "life eternal." The evidence of this is in doing "righteousness," which proves one is begotten of God.

PART II.
THE CHILDREN OF GOD AND CHILDREN OF THE DEVIL, 3:1—4:6.

God has children, 2:29. How did it come about?

1. The great love of God, 3:1, 2. "Behold," look, consider how great it is: (a) in quality, Rom. 5:8, 10; (b) in quantity, John 3:16; (c) in effect—"such we are" (now), cp. John 1:12, and in the resurrection we shall be like Christ, Phil. 3:21. Such love is almost incredible!

2. Distinction between children of God and those of the devil, 3:3-13.

a. The children of God strive against sin, 3-6. The hope of seeing Christ and being like Him is the motive for self-purification. The Christian was purified from past sins by "obedience to the truth," I Pet. 1:22; now he must "press on unto perfection" in the same manner, Heb. 6:1, cp. Ps. 119:11. This is essential, because he is constantly subject to sin, I John 1:8, and "sin is lawlessness" with penalty attached. In striving against sin, Christ is the model. He came "to take away sins; and in him is no sin." Therefore the one who abides in Him "sinneth not" willfully and habitually.

b. The children of the devil practice sin, 7-9. They deceive by false teaching, hence children of God must be on guard, cp. 2:26. They constantly commit sin, hence are of the devil, the originator and propagator of sin, whose kingdom ("works") and person, Heb. 2:14, are doomed to destruction by "the Son of

God." Note Gen. 3:15. Unlike the devil's children, God's child cannot sin deliberately, purposely, for two reasons: the gospel "seed," Luke 8:11, is in him and it prohibits sin; he is begotten of God, whose hereditary character is sinless.

Conclusion, 10-13. Right going and brotherly love differentiate the children of God from those of the devil. Hating a brother relates one to Cain, a murderer and son of the devil. This explains why the ungodly world hates God's children. See John 3:20; 15:18, 19.

3. Evidence of having passed out of death into life, 3:14-24. We are either in "death" or in "life." How can we know we are in life? "Hereby know we":

a. By love for the brethren. Hate is murder, as proved by Cain. How is this love known? It is manifest in deeds. Christ gave His life for us; and, if necessary, we should "lay down our lives for the brethren." Some have done that. It also calls for sharing "the world's goods" with a brother in need. Cp. Matt. 25:35-40. Thus we prove the love of God in us.

b. By voice of conscience. "If our hearts condemn us." The scriptural heart includes intellect, affections, will and conscience, and conscience speaks, Rom. 2:15. "God is greater" than we are in knowledge of our shortcomings, and His condemnation is greater than that of our conscience. "If our hearts condemn us not," then have we boldness toward God in prayer, "because we keep his commandments," namely, to believe in His Son and love one another.

The result from such living is companionship. We abide in Him and He in us through the Spirit, cp. John 14:23; recall I John 1:3.

4. Difference between truth and error, 4:1-6. To Christians is given the Spirit of God, 3:24. Opposed to them is "the spirit of antichrist." How detect the difference?

First, the ability to know, vs. 1. "Prove" (test) the teachers. The early church possessed the gift of "discerning of spirits," I Cor. 12:10, and, like Jesus, they could know "what was in man," John 2:25. Now we test the preachers and teachers by the word of God.

Second, the confession, vss. 2, 3. That marks the great difference—then and now. The true teacher spoke "by the Holy

Spirit," I Cor. 12:3, and he said "Jesus Christ is come in the flesh." The false teachers, moved by the spirit of antichrist, denied this, and it classified them as children of the devil (chap. 3).

Third, the victory, vss. 4-6. False teachers are "overcome" (defeated) already because of Him who said John 16:33b. They are of the world and speak that which the world supplies. "We [apostles] are of God," the source of our message. "By this we know" the difference between truth and error.

PART III.
THE SIGNIFICANCE OF LOVE AND FAITH, 4:7—5:17.

The spirit of the world has been shown to be hatred, murder and antichristian teaching, the source of which is the devil. Opposed to these are faith in Christ and love for one another, 3:23. Their importance occupies the rest of the epistle.

1. Exhortation to mutual love, 4:7-21.

a. The source of love, 7, 8. "Love is of God." Manifestation of it by the believers proves him to have been "begotten of God," for "God is love." Something divine has come into the true Christian, Rom. 5:5.

b. The example of love, 9-13. God's love for man is seen in sending Christ "that we might live through him," for He is "the propitiation [cover] for our sins." Since God "so loved us," we should love one another, an evidence that God lives "in us," cp. John 14:23. The fact of His indwelling is certified by the gift of "his Spirit," Acts 2:38b.

c. The life of love, 14-21. Love springs from Christ whom "we [apostles] have beheld," cp. 1:1, 2. It enters one who "shall confess that Jesus is the Son of God," cp. Matt. 16:16. The effect is fellowship. God lives in him, and he in God.

Love is "made perfect" by absence of fear of the coming "day of judgment," because "as he [Christ] is, so are we." We belong to Him (I Cor. 6:20); He lives in us (Gal. 2:20), and He will be our Judge (Acts 17:31). "Perfect love casteth out fear."

Finally, God's love becomes the motive of life. "We love, because he first loved us." Love for God and brethren is coexistent. He who professes love for God and hates his brother "is a liar," hence a son of the devil, John 8:44.

2. The life of faith in Christ, 5:1-17.

a. Faith and love, 1-3. God's children are distinguished by two facts: they are begotten of God by believing "Jesus is the Christ" and also "the Son of God," 4:15; they love, not only the begetter, but also the begotten believer—a token of love for God.

b. Faith and victory, 4, 5. The faith of the born-again believer fights the world, and victory is certain because he believes "that Jesus is the Son of God." The verb "hath overcome" is in the aorist tense, which indicates victory from the very beginning. Cp. Col. 1:6.

c. Faith and testimony, 6-12. That Jesus is the Son of God is confirmed by three witnesses describing Him. "This is he that came" is attested by:

(1) The *water* of His baptism, Matt. 3:15-17. It was an act of righteousness which called forth the Father's testimony concerning His Son.

(2) The *blood* of His atonement. It was shed for "remission of sins," Matt. 26:28, a fact which fits Jesus only and is witnessed by prophets and apostles, Isa. 53:5; I Pet. 2:24.

(3) The *Spirit* of truth. He descended upon Jesus at His baptism for the purpose of pointing Him out as "the Son of God," John 1:33, 34. Of the Spirit Jesus said, "he shall bear witness of me," John 15:26, which He did through the apostles. "Because the Spirit is the truth," therefore when He says Jesus is the Son of God His testimony is reliable.

These three witnesses are unanimous—they *"agree"* that Jesus is the Son of God. If we receive human testimony (and we do), God's testimony is *"greater."* The one who believes in His Son has the testimony in his heart, Rom. 10:10; the external witness has become internal certainty. The disbeliever makes God out to be a liar who is on record as the giver of eternal life in His Son. It follows that he who has the Son is alive, he who has Him not is dead.

d. Faith and prayer, 13-17. The purpose in writing was to assure believer of eternal life. This assurance results in confidence that prayer to God is heard and answered, if we ask "according to his will," cp. 3:22.

A special case. If a Christian brother is sinning not unto death, pray for him that he may have life. (In sin is death.) If he sins unto death, don't pray for him. What is that sin? It is knowable or there could be no distinction observed. Since "he that hath the Son hath life," vs. 12, the sin unto death is falling away from Christ, the life. It consists in a deliberate renunication of Him and embracing evil, a total apostasy. See Heb. 6:4-6 and note illustration following.

CONCLUSION, 18-21.

From this epistle "we know" three things:

1. The child of God and sin. The begotten of God does not sin deliberately; recall 3:6. He "keepeth himself" through definite antagonism to evil, cp. Jas. 4:7b. Moreover, the evil one cannot touch him, because he is guarded "by the power of God," I Pet. 1:5.

2. The child of God and the world. There is a difference. The former "is begotten of God," hence is "of God"; the world lies in (is completely controlled by) "the evil one."

3. The believer and the Son of God. He knows that the Son has actually come and has revealed the true God, consequently our life is in God and in Christ. This knowledge is life eternal, cp. John 17:3. With deepest paternal feeling the closing appeal is to guard against idols—images—since there is but one true God.

Second Letter of John

The letter is a brief personal note to an excellent Christian lady and her family. The purpose was to champion "the truth" and to advise her not to receive into her home deceptive tramp preachers who would impose upon her hospitality and thereby get recognition among the churches, saying they had been her guests and received her greeting.

ANALYSIS AND NOTES

1. Salutation, 1-3.

a. The writer. John designates himself as "The elder," meaning one "advanced in years," a title of dignity and respect which would induce obedience to what he wrote, note Job 32:7. In point of time John outlived by many years the other apostles.

b. The readers. It is addressed to "the elect lady and her children." The terms "elect lady," according to the Greek, mean an excellent lady of superior rank and character, who supported the church with her wealth and influence. Some think "lady" means church, but evidently it designates a woman, because she had children and a sister with children, vs. 13.

"Love" and "truth" caused John to write. He has been styled "the apostle of love," but he is more; he is the apostle of *love* and *truth,* the two inseparable characteristics of the gospel, a message which "shall be with us for ever." It is *"eternal* good tidings," Rev. 14:6.

c. The benediction, 3. Divine grace, mercy and peace are for the believer who lives "in truth and love." Who would not want that experience? A higher, more satisfactory plane of life is not imaginable. Paul puts it this way in II Cor. 13:14. That is the joyful experience of heaven on earth.

2. Entreaty concerning truth and love, 4-6. What makes the gospel preacher and teacher happy? Greatest joy had come to John because the lady's children were "walking in the truth" contained in the Father's commandment. They had been reared in Christian training, Eph. 6:4, and now they traveled in the path of God's word, Ps. 119:35. By the same token the gospel preacher and teacher now rejoice when God's children of the local church walk in the truth of God's word.

"And now I beseech thee." The entreaty is to "love one another," the evidence of walking in the truth of God's commandments and of being "begotten of God," I John 4:7. It is manifest, not merely in affectionate words, "but in deed and truth," I John 3:18.

3. Warning against false teachers, 7-11. Truth must be defended, "for many deceivers are gone forth." They were the same as those referred to in I John 2:18-22. As in those days, so now, only the apostles of Christ can effectively meet deceivers without compromise. So we hear Paul, Phil. 1:17; Gal. 2:4, 5, and Peter, II Pet. 3:17, and John. Their letters to the churches handle every form of skepticism and for all times. Infidelity has nothing new.

The warning reads, "Look to yourselves," and for three reasons:

First, "that ye lose not the things we [apostles] have wrought," that is, our teaching, your salvation and the future reward. There can be no greater loss, therefore "hold fast . . . ," Heb. 10:23.

Second, "whosoever goeth onward" (away from "the teaching of Christ") is without God, hence has "no hope," Eph. 2:12.

Third, "if any [false teacher] cometh unto you" give neither hospitality nor greeting, for in so doing you become a partner to "evil works." The Christian can have "no fellowship with the unfruitful works of darkness," Eph. 5:11. His fight is *for* God and *against* the devil.

4. Conclusion, 12, 13.

a. Reason for brevity, 12. The apostle's soon visit accounts for the shortness of the epistle. Then he would speak with her about "many things," probably matters concerning the false teachers—their names, character and conduct—which he thought best not to write in a letter. Incidentally, we learn that the letter was written, not on parchment, but on paper, yet it has been preserved. The visit would result in mutual joy—the high note of the gospel.

b. The greeting, 13. It is from the children of the elect sister. Their mother, like her sister, was a lady of social rank and excellent character whose chief interest, no doubt, was in the church.

Third Letter of John

INTRODUCTION.

This is another brief note from "the elder" to a Christian named Gaius. The main purpose is to commend him for his hospitality to passing preachers of the gospel and to warn him against an arrogant church boss named Diotrephes.

ANALYSIS AND NOTES

1. Inscription and best wishes, 1, 2. Five persons by name of Gaius are recorded in Acts and the epistles, but whether the one John addressed was one of these is not known, for the name was common among Romans.

As in the letter to the "elect lady," so in this one, *love* and *truth* are linked, vs. 1. Truth lives always, elicits admiration and affection, particularly in those who know and love the truth.

The apostle's wish for Gaius, vs. 2, is that material prosperity and physical health may correspond to the prosperity of his soul. It is Christian to gain wealth "for necessary uses," Titus 3:14, and to take good care of one's health, but do not overlook the soul's prosperity. This will take care of "the outward and inward man."

2. Joyful testimony, 3-8. John was made happy by report from brethren concerning Gaius on two accounts:

a. He was "walking in the truth," 3, 4. Another case of divine truth walking among men, cp. II John 4. It was the gospel leaven at work in the community, Matt. 13:33.

b. He extended hospitality, 5-8. Like the "elect lady" of the second epistle, Gaius "set foward" traveling evangelists. His home was a "preachers' hotel" which called forth the praise of the apostle. This was the manner of support of pioneer evangelism in apostolic times, hence we note Titus 3:13; Heb. 13:2. In like manner were the early preachers of the Restoration Movement enabled to sow "the seed of the kingdom." Those extending Christian hospitality are spoken of as "fellow-workers for the truth."

3. Warning against Diotrephes, 9-12. It appears that this unscrupulous man was a so-called "ruling elder" in the church to which Gaius belonged. He loved to have "pre-eminence among them," refused to acknowledge the authority of the apostle, withheld his letter to the church, spoke wicked words against him, refused hospitality to traveling evangelists, forbade members of the church to practice it, and withdrew fellowship from those who did. This reprobate John would discipline when he visited the church, which reminds us of Paul's message to the unruly element in the church at Corinth (I Cor. 10:2, 10, 11; 12:20). Let us not forget that the apostles are still in authority in the church in matters of teaching and discipline.

John's appeal to the church was not to imitate the evil Diotrephes but rather the good Demetrius, 11, 12. His good character and conduct were attested by all men, by the truth and by the apostle. That is endorsement enough for any Christian.

4. Conclusion, 13, 14. As in his letter to the "elect lady," John had much to say to Gaius but deferred it until he could speak "face to face"—lit., "mouth to mouth," implying mutual conversation. He closes with the benediction of "peace," the salutation of "friends" and his own salutation to friends.

The brief personal notes of the second and third epistles are of great value to the church now. They disclose the following:

1. The affectionate relation of the apostle and his co-laborers, both men and women. Faith in Christ does bind people together in happy fellowship (even with the apostles) loved and longed for.

2. The repeated emphasis upon "the truth." It is "love in truth," "know the truth," "walking in the truth." This emphasis was needed because "many deceivers are gone forth;" and they left many descendants who are with us this day. Some churches

are concerned with being broad-minded instead of being truth-minded.

3. The unruly conduct of some professed Christians. The early church had its half-converted and unconverted members as has the church now. They are always the trouble makers and too often are permitted to get away with it, to the detriment of the church and the dishonor of Christ.

Letter of Jude

INTRODUCTION.

1. The author. He describes himself as "a servant of Jesus Christ, and a brother of James." Like James, he was therefore "the Lord's brother," Gal. 1:19; cp. Matt. 13:55. Jude and Judas are synonymous.

2. The date. Nothing definite is available. Similarity to II Pet. 2, shows that the two epistles could not have been written independently. Early church Fathers testify that Peter and Paul suffered martyrdom at about the same time, or A.D. 68. That could be the approximate date of the letter by Jude. Nothing is known of the place of writing.

3. The readers. From the many references to Old Testament history, it may have been intended for Jewish Christians, although its teachings and warnings are applicable to all Christians and for all time.

4. The purpose. It is definitely stated in vss. 3, 4. Ungodly men who had come into the church were corrupting faith and morals. A minute description is given of these adversaries of the faith with certain judgment to come.

ANALYSIS AND NOTES

INTRODUCTION, 1-4.

1. Salutation, 1, 2. After the author has made himself known, he addressed his readers as:

"Called." See II Thess. 2:13, 14. The call is verbal and intelligent.

"Beloved." This is enjoyed *in* God the sphere, and *from* God the Father. Note I John 3:1. That grips the soul!

"Kept." God keeps believers for Jesus Christ as His permanent possession. They are His by purchase, I Cor. 6:20.

Blessed. "Mercy" is from God to needy humanity. "Peace" is the state of the forgiven soul, cp. Rom. 5:1. "Love" is the mutual relation between God and His children, I John 4:19.

2. Reasons for writing, 3, 4. Licentious, false teachers were already at work in the church, hence for some time the writer had been giving "all diligence," or had desired, to write them. Now time for action had come with reference to "our common salvation."

a. The exhortation, 3. "Contend" calls for a strenuous, verbal defense of the faith by the church. Cp. Titus 1:10, 11. "The faith" means that which has been divinely revealed for Christians to believe. And it was *"once for all delivered,"* hence is final and complete.

In the light of the New Testament the vast importance of the faith once for all delivered is seen in that it was: (1) for all time; (2) for all circumstances; (3) for all purposes; (4) for all people.

b. The occasion, 4. The ungodly intruders "crept in privily"— came into the church through a side door, i.e., by infiltration. Cp. Gal. 2:4. They had been predicted and their destiny of "condemnation" made known, hence the church was forewarned but did not heed. To gratify their lusts of the flesh and to get gain they even denied *"our only Master and Lord, Jesus Christ."* Such persons John calls "antichrists" and liars, I John 2:18, 22. Here is a frightful condition against which the church needs to to be on guard *now.*

PART I.
JUDGMENT ON THESE WICKED MEN, 5-16.

The argument is based on examples from Old Testament history.

1. Three examples of collective punishment, 5-10.
a. Unbelieving Israelites, Num. 13, 14.
b. Rebellious angels, cp. II Pet. 2:4.
c. Sodom and Gomorrah, Gen. 19:1-28.

"In like manner" these reprobates in the church are destined for "punishment of eternal fire." They defile the flesh, despise divine authority, rail at dignities—a thing Michael did not do even against the devil but left the matter with the Lord. Thus they act like creatures without reason and fit themselves for destruction.

2. Three examples of individual punishment, 11.

a. Cain, Gen. 4. His "way" was envy, hatred and murder, cp. I John 3:15. Some now in the church are traveling with Cain. I John 3:15.

b. Balaam, Num. 22:7, 21. Like him, these greedily abandon themselves to getting gain, overlooking I Tim. 6:9, 10.

c. Korah, Num. 16:1-3, 31-35. Envy and self-seeking led to rebellion against divine authority vested in Moses and Aaron. Terrifying punishment followed. Likewise in the church there was, even now is, rebellion in various forms against divine authority. Retribution is certain.

"These are they." In 12-16 their character and conduct are described in denunciatory language of intense indignation which shows that these immoral, false teachers are utterly incapable of good spiritual results.

PART II.
EXHORTATION, 17-23.

1. To "remember," 17-19. Not only Enoch, vs. 14, but also the apostles had predicted these wicked men. The church had forgotten. Will she do so now? Paul had much to say of a great apostasy, I Tim. 4:1-3; II Tim. 3:1-8; 4:1-4. Subsequent church history discloses the wicked innovations.

2. To build themselves up, 20, 21. This to be accomplished through *faith, prayer, love* and *hope* for the mercy of the Lord unto eternal life.

3. To have mercy, 22, 23. Three classes face Christians: (a) Doubters. They need convincing evidence for faith. (b) Those in fire. They are already like brands in hell fire and should be snatched out. (c) The fearful. Compassion for them must be exercised with fear of being defiled, like touching a leper. Even their moral garment must be hated.

BENEDICTION, 24, 25.

In thought and words it is the most sublime to be found in the New Testament. It is definitely related to the whole epistle. Ascription of praise is offered to *"the only God that is able"*:

1. To guard you. Like soldiers on guard, God faithfully keeps His children from falling through influence of evil men. Cp. I Pet. 1:5.

2. To present you (A.V.). The believer's destiny is God's glory and exceeding joy. Cp. I Thess. 5:23. A strong incentive to faithfulness.

3. To save you. God is "the Savior of *all* men," I Tim. 4:10 (by raising them from the grave, John 5:28, 29), but *"specially* them that believe," II Pet. 1:11. This He does "through Jesus Christ."

Therefore, "unto Him be glory, majesty, dominion and power": in the *past*—"before all time"; at the *present*—"and now"; in the *future*—"for evermore." "Amen."